1.50

THE STORY OF JESUS

THE
STORY OF JESUS

A Book for Young People

BY
BASIL MATHEWS

With Numerous Photographs by
THE AUTHOR

HARPER & BROTHERS PUBLISHERS
New York and London
1934

PRINTED IN THE UNITED STATES
OF AMERICA
H-I

PREFACE

THE welcome given to *A Life of Jesus*[1] has led teachers
and parents to ask the author, through the publishers,
to write the story again, but at half the length. This
book, *The Story of Jesus,* is the response to their desire.
It is an entirely new book, and in no way is it a shorter
version of the other volume. As that *Life* has been trans-
lated for boys and girls in Finland, Germany, and
Sweden, the author hopes that this smaller book may
reach youth speaking still other languages in other lands.

The whole story of the Life is told afresh and does not
take for granted any previous knowledge of Jesus. Many
of the descriptions of the background of his life, gathered during repeated travel in the land where he lived,
are necessarily omitted from this shorter book. The
author, however, has tried to concentrate into these
pages sufficient background to help readers to see clearly
the scenes in which Jesus faced his adventures and to
arrive at a richer, more lively understanding of him and
of what he did and said. That, indeed, has been the gain
that has come to the author through visiting those scenes
again and again in Palestine, Transjordania, Syria, and
Egypt, and through trying to live the life over again in
imagination on the spot. For all of us, however, the great
way—open to every one—of finding what he is, is to
follow him.

As in the *Life*, the author has followed the usage of
the English New Testament in using a small initial for
the personal pronouns referring to Jesus. The photographs reproduced were taken by the author in the lands
when preparing to write these books. Those who wish

[1] Harper & Brothers.

to know the view taken as to the books of the Bible that relate to the life of Jesus are referred to the appendixes of the larger book. There is no room here for discussing the evidence on which the author's narrative of difficult or disputed parts of the story is based. He has weighed the evidence, come to decisions, and then told the story as he sees it. He can only hope greatly that this book will send its readers to those four little books in the New Testament that come down to us across the centuries with their immortal living picture of the Light of the World.

BASIL MATHEWS

Boston University

CONTENTS

LIST OF ILLUSTRATIONS

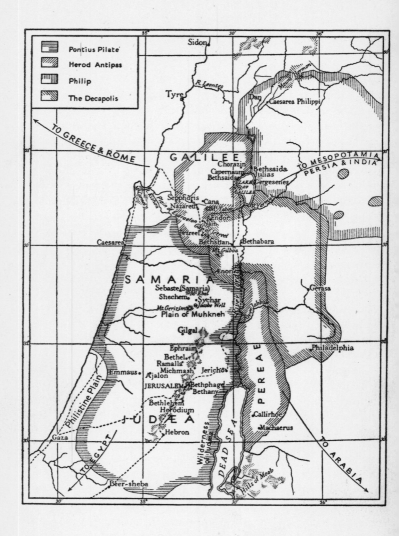

CHAPTER I

'A SON IS BORN'

'I HAVE no room; the place is full', said the innkeeper to the travel-stained man from the hill-country. He pointed, as he spoke, under the arch to the square court-yard already crowded with men tending their camels and donkeys. Through a farther doorway, Joseph could see the inn guest-room filled with the women-folk. All these people from many places had, like Joseph, travelled to Bethlehem because the Roman Emperor, Augustus, who ruled over that land, had ordered a list to be made of all the people in their own home-towns and villages.

The host's eyes moved from the face of Joseph to the tired girl seated on the donkey's back. For three days, with Joseph walking by her side, she had ridden south-ward over the stony hill-paths and down the valley-ways from Nazareth in Galilee to Bethlehem in Judaea. The man could see that she sorely needed rest and shelter.

'There is the stable,' he added, 'you can rest there if you wish.'

Thankful for even this, Joseph led the donkey into the stable. He helped Mary down and unfolded the bed-mats and woollen garments that had been her saddle. He then spread the mats upon the cleanest straw that he could find on the floor and wrapped her in a cloak. The inner half of the large chamber was the guest-room where a number of women were making their evening meal with their children. The floor of the guest-room was about two feet higher than that of the stable. Along the kerb-edge of the guest-room a deep manger was hollowed in the beaten and dried earth. Joseph shook some crushed straw and barley into this manger for the donkey's supper.

Joseph and Mary shared their meal, resting on the floor between the donkey and the oxen that were lying down chewing the cud. Gradually the noises of the men outside arguing and singing and of the women and children talking in the guest-room ceased. All were asleep. On the hill-slope outside, below the walls of Bethlehem, shepherds kept watch over their sheep in the folds, just as Joseph's ancestor, the shepherd-boy David, had done a thousand years earlier. The night was very still.

In the stable the quiet was broken by the first cry of a new-born baby. Mary's son was born. She opened a little roll that she had carried with her all the way from Nazareth in readiness for the coming of the child. Taking out a long, wide, woollen band she wound this swaddling-cloth about her first-born. With straw Joseph made him a resting-place in the manger. There she laid him. So they slept.

In the morning a group of men came hurrying along the street. Each carried a shepherd's crook and a strong cudgel. They were brown-faced, sturdy, bearded men, and had sheepskin cloaks flung over their shoulders. They asked the people in the street where it was that a baby had been born in Bethlehem that night. Soon they were directed to the inn. Entering the stable they saw the young mother, Mary, on her mat-couch, and Joseph standing by her. Swiftly their eyes turned to the manger to look at the baby. Mary and Joseph wondered what had brought them there in such haste. This is the story that the spokes-man of the shepherds told:

'We were in the fields keeping watch over our flock by night. A Messenger from God stood by us. The glory of the Lord shone round about us. We were much afraid. The Messenger said to us: "Be not afraid; for, behold, I bring you good tidings of great joy which shall be to all the people. There is born to you this day in the city of David a Saviour, which is the Lord, the Anointed. This

A stable, such as that at Bethlehem

is the sign. You shall find a babe wrapped with swaddling-clothes and lying in a manger." '

'Suddenly,' the shepherd went on, 'there was with the Messenger a multitude of the heavenly host praising God and saying: "Glory to God in the highest, and on earth peace among men of goodwill." So when the angels were gone away, we said to one another: "Let us go now to Bethlehem and see this thing that has happened." So we came with haste.'

Those who heard this wondered at what the shepherds said. Mary stored the words in her memory. The picture came back to her of how, months ago, in her own home in Nazareth, when she was alone, the voice of a Messenger of God had spoken to her also, saying: 'Hail, for thou art highly favoured: God is with thee.'

She had been greatly troubled at this saying and wondered what this greeting might mean, and the Messenger had said:

'Fear not, Mary, for thou hast found favour with God and shalt have a son. Thou shalt call his name Jesus. He shall be great, and shall be called the Son of the Most High. And the Lord God shall give unto him the throne of his father David. Of his kingdom there shall be no end.'

That was, indeed, a strange saying. For, on the throne of David, King over Jerusalem and all the land round about, was Herod the Great, a cruel, crafty tyrant nearly seventy years old. He had been made King by the Senate in Rome over thirty years before. To secure his position he had built seven castles, north, south, east, and west. These great citadels he garrisoned with soldiers to overawe the people. He had even killed his wife, Mariamne, and two of his sons, because he suspected that they were plotting to take his throne from him. What would he not do if he heard that a baby-boy was born of whom men said that he was to rule over Israel? The baby Jesus was only six miles away from Herod's palace in Jerusalem. And Herod had spies everywhere, listening for plots against him; for he knew that he was not loved. When word came to him of the birth of Jesus, he at once made up his mind to kill him.

The news came to Herod in this way. Three men rode on their camels through one of the arched gateways of Jerusalem at the end of a long journey from the high table-lands of Persia. They were Magi, learned in the knowledge of the stars. Why had they come a thousand miles all down the steep paths from Persia across the broad waters of the Euphrates river and over the desert sands of Arabia to cross the Jordan river and climb the rocky hills of Judaea into Jerusalem? This was naturally the question that camel-men and merchants asked the three Wise Men from the East as they sat round the night-fire in the inn court-yard at Jerusalem. They replied with another question.

'Where', they asked, 'is he that is born King of the Jews? We saw his star at its rising and we are come to worship him.'

Men everywhere believed that if a strange star or flaming comet appeared, or if the planets came near one another in the night-sky, it meant that a mighty king or great leader was to be born. These men gazing into the sky in Persia had seen a strange star rising. 'What great king is coming on the earth?' they asked each other eagerly. In those days men were talking of the expected coming of a new King of the Jews. For the Jews, scattered across many lands from the shores of the Atlantic Ocean in Gaul and Spain to the highlands of Persia and the Nile-cities of Egypt, sang and dreamed of the mighty Deliverer, whom God had, through their Seers, promised to send. This Messiah, as they called him—or, when they spoke in Greek, the Christ (the Anointed)—would, they hoped and prayed, free them from the rule of the Roman Emperor and his subject, King Herod. He would set up the Rule of God over all the world, with its centre in Jerusalem where the Messiah would reign on the throne of David. The Wise Men decided that the Deliverer shown by the star would be this new King. They set out to the capital city of the Jews on their long quest. In Jerusalem they asked in all innocence: 'Where is he that is born King of the Jews?' Herod's spies dashed off at once to him with the news. It roused him to instant action.

'Call to me the chief priest,' he commanded, 'with his learned men.'

When they arrived and stood before him, Herod asked what was to them a very simple question, for it was one that they often studied.

'Tell me,' he asked, 'where do your prophets say that the Christ is to be born?'

The scholars of the Law of Moses and of the Prophets replied at once, quoting the prophet Micah from memory. 'He will be born in Bethlehem in Judaea, for thus it is written by the prophet:

> "And thou, Bethlehem, land of Judah,
> Art in no wise least among the princes of Judah:
> For out of thee shall come a governor,
> Who shall be shepherd of my people Israel." '

'You may go,' said Herod. Hardly had they left him when he gave an order to another of his officers. 'Go and bring the Wise Men to me. But bring them secretly so that no one shall know.'

Soon they stood before him. After he had asked them when and where the star had appeared, he said: 'Go to Bethlehem, and search out carefully there concerning the young child. When you have found him, bring me word, that I also may come and worship him.'

So at night they mounted their camels. Coming out through the deep arch of the Jerusalem city gate, they went down the six miles of winding road, south-south-west to Bethlehem. They were excited and happy when at last they were led into the inn where Joseph and Mary were with the boy. Here—and not in the Palace of King Herod at Jerusalem—they bowed down with their foreheads to the floor, and they took out gifts that they had carried with them. These presents stood for riches, adoration, and health. They gave Jesus the precious metal, gold, mined by the hands of Africans; frankincense, a gum taken from the bark of a tree in Central India and used for burning in worship; and myrrh, a medicine from a shrub that grew in the desert places of Arabia.

Their quest completed, the Wise Men turned with light hearts to go home. As they rested in the inn at Bethlehem a dream came to them which they were sure meant that they were not to obey Herod's command to go back into Jerusalem and to tell him exactly where he might find the boy. But to disobey Herod was dangerous. So they went as fast as they could eastward, avoiding the great castle, Herodium, on the hill near Bethlehem, and avoiding Jericho, where he also kept a large garrison. They only breathed freely when, having forded the Jordan river, they climbed the hills into the East safe from King Herod's clutches. They were safe; but what of the child? Word quickly reached Herod that the Magi had sped homeward, disobeying his order. Angry at being foiled, he sent soldiers hot-foot along the track from Jerusalem, with orders to kill every boy-child in Bethlehem of two years of age and under.

Joseph, however, had grown anxious as he thought over the flight of the Wise Men and realized the peril that threatened the child. As he slept he, too, dreamed. 'Arise,' came the message, 'and take the young child and his mother, and flee into Egypt, and be thou there until I tell thee; for Herod will seek the young child to destroy him.'

Joseph wasted no time. While it was still dark he and Mary hurriedly got together food for the journey. Making a saddle of the mats, and wrapping Mary in a woollen cloak against the cold night-air, he set her on the back of the donkey, placed the boy in her arms, and took to the road. The donkey trotted sure-footed through the darkness down the stony ways. By dawn they were in the valleys. There Joseph found a hiding-place for rest and sleep during the day. The next night brought them to the city on the edge of the desert.

Taking all the food and drink that they could carry, ploughing through blown sand, sheltering under a rock-wall, or, when they could, under the date-palms of an oasis beside its well, they set their faces always west for weeks of hard travel. At last a rim of green showed on the horizon against the setting sun. It was the eastern edge of the delta of the River Nile. Here all the land was flat, with the black earth brought down through the centuries from the heart of Africa on the floods of the Nile, so unlike the high limestone hills and terraced vineyards of the land of Jesus' birth.

One afternoon Joseph and Mary could see in the distance the roofs of an Egyptian city. It was called the City of the Sun, Heliopolis. In that city of Egyptians was a quarter where the Jews lived. Here Joseph could find house-room. He was a building-carpenter by trade, so he could earn food, clothing, and shelter for Mary and the boy Jesus. Yet they could not think of this as really 'home'. Joseph longed for his carpenter's shop and his tools in Nazareth, and Mary wanted to see the faces of her friends at the well and to talk with them when grinding the wheat or barley for the cooking.

Herod fell ill; and in the spring-time, just before the great Feast of the Passover, he died. The news was brought by the camel-caravans of merchants to Egypt. Joseph's longing for home was on him. He dreamed that another message was given to him, saying: 'Arise and take the young child and his mother, and go into the land of Israel: for they are dead that sought the young child's life.'

It took them little time to prepare for the return journey. They faced again the weeks of travel across the desert, when Joseph must have told Jesus the story of how Moses had led his people, Jesus' people, the Hebrews, out of Egyptian slavery toward the land where Jesus himself was born. When they had crossed the desert and begun to climb the hills of Judaea they heard the news of the most recent happenings.

'Archelaus, the son of Herod, is reigning over Judaea in place of his father,' the people told Joseph. 'He is very cruel. Rebels revolted against him in Jerusalem at the Passover time. He sent his soldiers in and slew three thousand of them.'

As Joseph pondered this bad news, it was a relief to him to think that the rule of Archelaus was only over Judaea and did not stretch over Nazareth in the highlands of Galilee in the north. Again he was guided by a dream, and he led Mary and the boy by the sea-side northward. Keeping to the sea-plain, they avoided the hills of Judaea on the right. On the left they could see the shining blue Mediterranean Sea and in the harbour of Caesarea, within the mighty mole that Herod had built, ships from Rome. They were now only a day's walk from home.

They took the very narrow strip of coast between the great head of Mount Carmel and the sea, and then they followed the road as it turned inland. Boulders in the bed of the little River Kishon made stepping-stones for them all to cross by. Then they began to climb the little hills that lead to the Galilee highlands. The path was steeper and steeper winding up the hills. They crested the ridge: their home lay before them.

The boy looked down for the first time into the lovely basin in the hills that held the house in which he was to live, the workshop where he was to learn his trade as a carpenter, the streets where he would play with the other children. This town was to be his home till he should grow to be a man.

CHAPTER II

THE HOME AMONG THE HILLS

JOSEPH, Mary, and their small son went quickly down the steep Nazareth street.

'Shalom,'—'Peace be with you,'—called one friend after another in greeting as they passed the little booths open to the street, where the copper-smith and the saddler, the corn-merchant, the potter and the weaver, sat reckoning their day's trade before closing for the night.

They stopped before a small square house built of rough-hewn stone from the hills. This was their home. The donkey trotted into the little courtyard at the side, from which stone steps, outside the wall of the house, led up to the flat roof. Joseph threw open the door. As he did so he touched a folded parchment fixed by a leather cover to the door-post. Then he put to his lips the fingers that had touched the parchment. He lifted Jesus up to do the same and repeated the verses written on the parchment:

'Hear, O Israel: the Lord our God is one Lord: and thou shalt love the Lord thy God with all thine heart and with all thy soul and with all thy might.'

Although Jesus was only three or four years old, he had already learned these words by heart. They were the first lines that a child was taught to repeat.

That parchment was placed there on the door-post, Joseph explained to Jesus, because the commandment in the Scroll of Deuteronomy said: 'And thou shalt write these words upon the posts of thy house, and on thy gates.'

Mary now led Jesus into the house. It had only one room. The floor was of earth beaten flat with mallets. It was dark there, for the few windows were small and high up in the thick walls. So Mary took a jar from a hollow in the wall, poured oil from it into the little flat narrow

The Virgin's Well, Nazareth

earthenware hand-lamp, and lighted the wick. She set this lamp on a strong pillar of wood which stood in the room, the lamp-stand, so that it should give light to the house. From a wooden chest she drew out the woven rugs that were their beds. These were usually rolled up in the day-time out of the way on a broad shelf shaped in the wall itself. On a little table only a few inches high, Mary set cheese and bread and olives for supper. Before they sat down on the floor by this table, she poured water from a jar with a small spout over the hands of each of them. This would be Jesus' task when he grew a little older, for it was always the work of the youngest in the family. Joseph then spoke a prayer, asking God's blessing on them and thanking Him for the food. So they took their evening meal and lay down to sleep.

Early in the morning Joseph rose and went out, eager to get to the work that he had left for so long. When Mary started out with her tall earthenware jar down the street to the well-spring, Jesus walked with her. All the younger women and older girls of Nazareth came to the spring that gushed out of the hill-side, for it was the one source of water for drinking and for cooking in the town. Mary, as one of the young wives of Nazareth, found many friends there. After they had talked she filled her jar, and, balancing it on her head, walked home with graceful steps.

When they reached home, Jesus followed her out into the courtyard where she sat on the ground by a little hand-mill. Two flat, round stones, shaped like wheels, about eighteen inches across, lay one on top of the other. An axle fixed into the centre of the lower stone came up through the centre of the upper one. Mary seized a wooden handle fixed into the top stone, and with it, helped by a neighbour, she turned the stone round and round. She poured grain slowly through the hole in the middle of the top stone. So it was gradually ground into flour, which came trickling out between the two stones all round the edges.

This flour Mary gathered up into a basin, and moistened with a little water. Going to her supply of yeast or leaven, she took a little and thrust it in. While the yeast was working, Mary went to a funnel-shaped mound of earth in the courtyard and stooped to enter a small doorway in its side. Under a curved lid was a hollow circle over two feet deep, with pebbles and broken bits of tile and crockery at the bottom. Replacing the lid she spread dried dung and twigs of shrubs on it and set the fuel alight. It burned slowly with a warm glow. While it burned she made dough of the flour and patted it into flat, circular pieces, like pancakes. At last the glow died down and only ashes remained. Lifting the lid, she, with a swift, deft movement, slapped the flat, thin dough cakes on to the hot tiles and pebbles and quickly replaced the lid. In a short time the loaves were cooked. If Jesus asked about the leaven, as we may be sure he did, Mary would explain that it was the leaven, working secretly inside the flour, that made it good to eat. With cheese and olives, grapes from the hill-side or figs from their own tree, or perhaps dates brought by camel across the desert, Jesus and his parents made their simple, pleasant meal.

At the end of the meal it was simple to wash the few dishes. Mary showed how wrong it was to wash the outside of the basin and not be sure that the inside was cleansed. One day Joseph and a friendly neighbour carried home a long wooden chest with a lid made to fit so closely that the silvery fish-moths could not enter. For it was to be a clothes chest, to hold the Sabbath robe with its blue tassels and Mary's special garment for weddings. On that garment were silver ornaments. One had to be careful that no thief broke in to steal them. This had happened with one of the neighbours. There was no place so secure that neither moth nor rust could eat away your precious things, nor thieves come and steal.

Upon her forehead Mary wore a beautiful string of ten silver coins—a part of her dowry on her betrothal and marriage. One day the thread with which they were sewn on broke; one of them fell off and rolled into a dark place. She was troubled at losing this part of the family treasure and she told her neighbours about it. She lit her little hand-lamp and with her twig-besom swept the earthen floor till at last, with a cry of joy, she saw the light glint on the lost piece of silver. She was happier about the piece that was lost and found than about all the others.

In after years Jesus used these little events in the daily life of his home in his parables.

Jesus had no books, but as he grew up he heard from Joseph and Mary tales of the great men and women of his people. He could picture the old patriarchs, Abraham and those who came after him, riding on their camels, with their flocks and herds, and their servants pitching their long, low, goat-hair tents by the water-springs.

Mary no doubt told him the stories of the women of the Hebrew people: Rebekah lifting the tent-flap of her father's home and going to water the camels at the fountain, and being chosen to be the bride of Isaac; the undying love of Ruth for Naomi; the glory of the brave wise woman, Deborah, who sent her soldiers down the defile near Nazareth to drive the armies of Sisera in headlong defeat, and who, sitting under her oak-tree, judged the people for many years. Jesus heard how Rebekah's sons, Esau and Jacob, quarrelled and made it up again; and again, later on, how Jacob, as an old man, was horrified to see his favourite son's coat of many colours all blood-stained, although really young Joseph had only been thrown into a pit by his angry brothers who sold him to the slave-dealers to be carried down to the palaces of Pharaoh in Egypt.

So the enthralling story went on. Jesus learnt how the great men of long ago, taught by God, led the people in the struggle with their enemies, forming these wandering tribes into a great nation. He heard how the cruel Egyptian task-masters lashed the toiling Israelites, until Moses, the baby who had rocked on the Nile waters in his cradle of rushes, grew to manhood, and God called him to lead the Hebrew people, as they were now called, out of Egypt. He heard how the chariots and horsemen of Pharaoh galloped to their destruction in the Red Sea, and how, after years of weary wandering in the desert, the people at last crested the hills from which the Promised Land could be seen. There the brave general, Joshua, took up Moses' task and led the people over Jordan to climb the rocky valleys into Canaan.

The boys and girls were saddened by the tragic story of the strong man, Samson, who, though so mighty in thew and muscle, was not so strong in his will and self-control; so that he became the blinded slave of the Philistines; until, chained between pillars to be the butt of three thousand jeering feasters, he thrust the great wooden tree-trunks asunder and brought the hall crashing in upon himself and the mocking crowd.

Mary would rather tell the story of how the boy Samuel's mother led him to the Temple to wait upon the old priest, Eli, little dreaming that Samuel would himself grow to be the wisest of all the judges of the people, and would by and by anoint tall handsome Saul as King, and then the greatest ruler that the Jews have ever known. This was David, whose friendship with Jonathan, and whose adventures with the lion and the bear, in the fight with Goliath, and in the service of Saul, make one of the most dramatic stories of the world. His son, Solomon, in the city that David created from a Jebusite fort, the City of Peace—Jerusalem—built the first of the marvellous temples, the last of which, built by Herod the Great, was even now barely finished.

The story was not ended. The Hebrew people were still struggling A boy could still look forward to serving his people as a leader. Jesus' nation owned the greatest treasure in the world; they alone among all the nations in that day knew that God is One, that He is Good; that He is Merciful. Yet they did not do His Will. And they were under the rule of the Roman Empire. Every coin that Joseph earned and that Jesus took when he went to buy things for his mother, had on one side of it the head of the Emperor. The Romans exacted many taxes from the Jews. Joseph in Nazareth, like all his fellow countrymen, had to pay a salt-tax, a town-tax, a house-tax, a road-tax, a tax on meat, and even on the water from the fountain. But, in return for these taxes, the strong hand of Rome brought them great good: the pirates on the seas, and robbers on the roads, were suppressed; good roads ran straight across the lands, and much trading between the peoples made merchants rich. A nation, however, like the Jews, who believed that they were the chosen people of God, could not be happy under the rule of any other people, still less a heathen power like the Romans. What should a Jewish boy who wanted in that day to serve God and his nation hope to grow up to be?

Some hot-headed zealots longed to lead a rebellion against the Romans. Joseph and Mary, however, and multitudes of Jews like them all over the world, had another vision of the future. They dreamed and talked of a Deliverer who would come and bring in the Golden Age of the Reign of God. Joseph would repeat from memory from the Scroll of Daniel:

'The God of Heaven shall set up a Kingdom
Which shall never be destroyed.

.   .   .   .

The Kingdom and the dominion,
And the greatness of the Kingdom under the whole heaven,
Shall be given to the people of the Saints of the Most High:

His Kingdom is an everlasting Kingdom,
And all dominions shall serve and obey him.'

That was the Kingdom; but who was to bring it in? Jesus, as a boy, was stirred as he learned by heart the words of the Scroll of Isaiah:

'The people that walked in darkness
Have seen a great light:
They that dwell in the land of the shadow of death,
Upon them hath the light shined . . .
For unto us a child is born,
Unto us a son is given,
And the government shall be upon his shoulder:
And his name shall be called Wonderful,
Counsellor, the Mighty God, the Everlasting Father,
The Prince of Peace.
Of the increase of his government and peace
There shall be no end,
Upon the throne of David, and upon his kingdom,
To order it, and to establish it
With judgement and with justice
From henceforth even for ever.'

If that son was to be—as the Prophet's Scroll said—'the Prince of Peace', he could not be a warrior leading a revolt. As Jesus listened in the synagogue to the reading of the still lovelier words about the Servant-Messiah, he felt them move his heart strangely:

'Behold my servant, whom I uphold;
Mine elect in whom my soul delighteth;
I have put my spirit upon him:
He shall bring forth justice to the Nations.

He shall not cry nor lift up
Nor cause his voice to be heard in the street.
A bruised reed shall he not break,
And the smoking flax shall he not quench.
He shall bring forth judgement with truth.
He shall not fail, nor be discouraged,
Till he have set judgement in the earth:
And the isles shall wait for his law.'

At last the reader came to words that rang like a trumpet in the ears of the boy, with their call to put all his heart and soul into altering the lives of men. No other words in all the Scrolls of the Law and of the Prophets called to him as these did. In them he saw what his life must be.

> 'The Spirit of the Lord God is upon me;
> Because the Lord hath anointed me
> To preach good tidings unto the meek;
> He hath sent me to bind up the broken-hearted,
> To proclaim liberty to the captives,
> And the opening of the prison to them that are bound;
> To proclaim the acceptable year of the Lord,
> And the day of vengeance of our God:
> To comfort all that mourn:
> To appoint unto them beauty for ashes,
> The oil of joy for mourning,
> The garment of praise for the spirit of heaviness;
> That they might be called trees of righteousness,
> The planting of the Lord, that he might be glorified.
> And they shall build the old wastes.
> They shall raise up the former desolations.
> And they shall repair the waste cities,
> The desolations of many generations.'

One night in the winter, although it was cold, the boys and girls hurried after dark to the roofs of their homes. All up the curving hill-side the roofs of the houses twinkled with lights. Up and down the streets older boys and young men marched, singing and waving torches. Every lamp in Nazareth was alight. It was the first of the eight days of the Feast of Lights.

As they sat on the roof wrapped in woollen cloaks, Joseph told them the story of this Feast of Lights, often called the Feast of the Dedication of the Temple. The Jews had been ruled a hundred and fifty years ago, he said, by a Syrian king, Antiochus Epiphanes. He cared nothing for our God or for His holy Temple. Then the great soldier, Judas Maccabeus, led the Hebrews into battle. They conquered the tyrant, and Maccabeus set up the throne of David in Jerusalem. With many services of cleansing he purified the old Temple; all over the world the Hebrews rejoiced, and they came from every land again to worship there. So every year now, at the time when Judas Maccabeus cleansed the Temple, the Feast of Lights was celebrated.

A few months later, in the early spring, the noisiest of all the feasts was held. It was also the most patriotic feast; for it celebrated the wonderful way Queen Esther foiled the plot of crafty, cunning Haman, who tried to get the Persian King Xerxes to massacre the whole nation of the Jews. The story was read aloud to all the people in the synagogue from the Book of Esther. The boys stamped on the floor when the name of Haman was read out, crying: 'Let his name be blotted out, the name of the wicked shall rot.' They shouted with glee when the reader told how the King gave the order, 'Hang Haman on the gallows that he set up for Mordecai'. So they all went home for a joyful feasting.

CHAPTER III

THE PILGRIMAGE TO JERUSALEM

THE greatest of all the festivals came next. It was held in the first month of the Jewish year, called 'The Month of Ears', because then the ears of wheat begin to grow. This Feast of the Passover celebrated God's wonder-work when He freed the Israelites from the tyrant Pharaoh. From Gaul and Spain, Greece and Egypt, the shores of the Black Sea and the tablelands of Persia, Jews trudged and sailed to Jerusalem, sometimes two million strong, to celebrate this feast, when unleavened bread was eaten to recall how their forefathers in Egypt had had to hasten away without time to let the yeast ferment.

Every year, as a small boy, Jesus watched the pilgrims start off from Nazareth for the three days' tramp southward to Jerusalem to the Feast of the Passover. When would the day come, he wondered, as he saw the procession trail off over the hills, when he himself would be old enough to go? At his thirteenth birthday Jesus would become, like all Jewish boys, 'a Son of the Law'. Up till that time a boy's father was responsible for what he did. But at the age of thirteen a boy was held by the rabbis to be responsible himself for his actions. To celebrate that important stage in a boy's life his parents would always try to take him up to Jerusalem to 'the Feast'. Jesus' parents decided to take him to Jerusalem for the Passover before his thirteenth birthday.

It was a long tramp for a twelve-year-old boy; eighty miles of walking over stony hills, through winding valleys, across the wide plain. But Jesus was a sturdy boy. Good simple food of cheese and bread, olives and figs; playing and walking in the open air of the Galilean hills; helping in the carpenter's shop, where he carried and held planks for his father and was learning to use the hammer, the chisel, and the saw; all this toughened his muscles and made him healthy. So Jesus was able to take that long journey.

There were, however, other reasons why he was fit to go to the Feast. He was an all-round boy. Not only was his body strong; his mind was swift and eager; his spirit was quick to learn. For, as those who told Luke of Jesus' boyhood said, he was 'filled with wisdom; and the grace of God was upon him'. Jerusalem, with the Temple, was the University as well as the centre of worship for the whole Jewish people. Jesus was now of an age to learn what was taught by the scribes and the rabbis there.

At last the longed-for day broke. Joseph and Mary were up early preparing for the journey; but Jesus was already up and about. With a bag stuffed with bread and other food, the travelling water-pot filled, and the mats on the donkey's back, they set out for the fountain where all gathered for the journey. The rabbi gave the signal to start. 'Peace be with you,' cried the friends to one another. Camels and donkeys; rabbis, farmers, and merchants; men and women and boys—the many-coloured pilgrimage of old and young moved slowly through the street to the south up the hill and over the crest.

As Nazareth fell out of sight, Jesus, looking southward, saw the wide, sunny spaces of the Plain of Esdraelon, green with the early shoots of the barley harvest; and farther away on the west the brave mass of Mount Carmel like a resting lion, and to the east the sharp sugar-loaf of Mount Tabor, with the gap through which the way led steeply down eastward into the Jordan Valley. But, as Joseph would explain, they were going straight to the south through those tumbled hills of Samaria, which Jesus could see in the distance.

They walked quickly down the steep ways from the Nazareth hills into this Plain. On and on they tramped between the barley fields, resting at midday for food and to snatch a short sleep before doing the last part of the day's journey. When the afternoon shadows lengthened they were on the south side of the Plain of Esdraelon. Ahead of them the valley opened into the hills of Samaria. Here Jesus gazed on the faces of men of Damascus who had trailed on camel-back for weeks across the deserts of the east from Persia and from the banks of the Tigris and the Euphrates. Their path now joined that of the Nazareth pilgrims. They were all bound for the Feast. Together they camped for the night. Jesus helped to make a hut of branches under which his mother could sleep. After evening prayer he lay down on his small mat-bed under the stars. Not all the howling of hungry jackals around the camp could keep awake this boy tired with the long day's tramp.

In the morning they started through the land of the Samaritans. The Samaritans hated the Jews, and Jewish travellers from Galilee to Jerusalem often turned away to the east at this point instead of taking the direct way to Jerusalem, through the hills of Samaria, so that they would not be in danger of being attacked and killed. They plunged down the steep ways through the Gap of Jezreel into the Jordan Valley and marched southward to Jericho, where they turned again to the west and climbed the hills of Judaea to Jerusalem.[1] But the boy Jesus was in a great body of pilgrims with many strong young men among them whom the Samaritans would be afraid to attack. So these pilgrims were not afraid to take the straight road through Samaria.

Joseph could point out to Jesus the Valley of Dothan as they passed by; for there his namesake, the boy Joseph, was thrown into a pit and sold to the passing merchants. On the left on a splendid hill were the shining pillars of

[1] See map.

a new justice-hall, a theatre, and palace-citadel which
Herod the Great had built only a few years before Jesus
was born. This was Sebaste, the capital of Samaria.

Towards sunset Jesus saw two great mountains casting
their shadows across the land. 'Those are the Mounts of
Blessing and of Cursing,' he was told. Joshua had led the
people of Israel across the Jordan and up the valley to this
very place. There one part of the people on the slopes of
Mount Ebal shouted the curses that would fall on those
who did not obey the Law given by Jehovah to Moses,
and the other part of the people, on the slopes of Mount
Gerizim, cried out the blessings of the obedient.

On the very crest of Mount Gerizim Jesus could see a
noble temple. It was only here, said the Samaritans, that
God could be rightly worshipped, and not in Jerusalem.
So Jesus walked with the pilgrims along the road between
these mountains to a clump of trees. They had now come
to the southern edge of Samaria, having walked through
it from north to south during the day.

'There is the well of our father, Jacob,' cried the old
rabbi to the younger pilgrims who were making the journey
for the first time. Jesus listened while the rabbi told the
story of how the great sheikh, Jacob, seventeen hundred
years earlier, when leading his thousands of sheep and
goats and his hundreds of camels along this way, had dug
this deep well. He did so in order to provide water for
his family, his shepherds and herdsmen, his flocks and his
herds, independent of the bad-tempered sheikhs of the city
of Shechem, who grumbled at letting him have the use of
their springs and water-courses.

Jesus watched the leather water-bucket being let down
and down on a rope more than eighty feet into the dark
depths of this well. He would be eager to help to pull it up
brimming with sparkling, pure, cold water for the pilgrims
tired and thirsty with their long day's walk. After another

night's rest here, at dawn the long caravan of pilgrims again took the road. Crossing the open fruitful valley of the cornfields—the Plain of Mukhneh—Jesus climbed the steep boulder-strewn track that wound upward towards the harsh grey ridges of the hills of Judaea. When they stopped to rest at the top he looked down ravines that fell to his left eastward to the River Jordan and on his right westward to the Great Sea.

The stories that he had heard at home from his parents came alive again here. For he could see on a stony hill-crest on his left the very village where King Saul was born. Indeed, up that ravine on his right the Philistines had fought their way against King Saul when he was encamped at Michmash and at Gilgal,[1] only to be driven back in panic down to the sea.

On another hill-top on the left of the road Joseph pointed out the hill that Jacob had called Bethel, or the House of God, because when he was fleeing from the anger of his brother Esau, he lay down to rest with his head on a stone and dreamed that he saw the ladder with angels going up and down between earth and heaven.

All these places, however, were forgotten when, coming round a curve at a shoulder in the hills, Jesus saw the afternoon sun flashing on the white walls of Jerusalem. Here was the goal of the pilgrimage. And when he saw it, Jerusalem was more marvellously beautiful than it had ever been before, with the glorious new Temple that Herod the Great had built, his great Palace-Citadel and open-air Theatre, and the towering walls.

Now all talking ceased in the caravan. They had come to the place where the Galilean pilgrims always turned away to the left to climb the Mount of Olives to their regular camping-ground. Some one started the psalm that Jesus and all the boys and other pilgrims knew—the

[1] Follow with the map.

Song of Ascents. So he joined with them all in the joyful words:

> 'I was glad when they said unto me
> Let us go unto the house of the Lord.
> Our feet shall stand within thy gates,
> O Jerusalem.'

Thus Jesus came for the first time to the ridge of the Mount of Olives—looked at Jerusalem across the deep ravine of the Kidron. He could see the rays of the setting sun glinting from the shield and helmet of the Roman soldier on sentry-go on the parapet of the Tower of Antony which crowned the city's western hill. From that high tower the sentinel could look down into the vast courts of the Temple where already many thousands of pilgrims moved to and fro; and could sound the alarm and summon the special Temple guard if a riot broke out.

All around the boy Jesus was a hubbub of noise and endless movement. For hundreds of thousands of people, sometimes in those days over a million people, came to Jerusalem to the Feast of the Passover. They camped on the hills around Jerusalem and crowded its narrow streets. Here were some bearded Jews who had sailed from the western end of the Great Sea to the eastern end; and men from far-away Spain, where the pillars of Hercules opened on the Atlantic Ocean. Behind them was a swarthy merchant who had come on his camel from Persia, almost as far away to the east as Spain was to the west. A Jew from far up the Nile Valley in Africa was listening to the strange story told by a brother Hebrew from Gaul about a voyage he had made across a narrow sea channel in the far north to the savage British tribes, who painted themselves blue and lived on an island which the Roman legions had begun to conquer. So the boy Jesus, straight from his little country town, rubbed elbows with men and women and boys of his nation from many lands. This young

The Temple Area, Jerusalem, from the Mount of Olives

lawyer hailed from the broad plains of the Danube; that expert weaver of tent-cloth from the high tableland of Asia Minor; those cloth merchants came, one from the banks of the Tigris, and the other from the banks of the Rhone. This dealer in furs had sailed from the wharves of Brundisium, in the Adriatic, and that rabbi from facing Greek philosophers on the streets of Athens; while yonder farmer had trudged from the almond groves above Smyrna; and that scholar, with a scroll under his arm, came from the university of Alexandria in Egypt.

To all of them Jerusalem was the centre of the world. What drew them was not Herod's massive citadel, or lovely palace with its gardens, or marble theatre—all of which Jesus could see from the Mount of Olives—a hundred cities in the Roman Empire could show finer sights than these. The power that drew the Jewish people was the belief that under that golden roof which, for the boy Jesus that afternoon, reflected the last rays of the setting sun, was the Holy Place where the very Splendour of the God of Abraham and Isaac and Jacob, the Shekinah of the Eternal, rested. There, and there alone, could sacrifice be made for the forgiveness of a man's sins; there was the world-centre for the worship of the True God.

As Jesus lay down to sleep he could hear pilgrims singing the songs about the city and her Temple that he had himself learned by heart. They chanted the words sung by Jews all over the world in the worship of God:

> 'I will worship toward thy holy Temple
> And praise thy name for thy loving kindness,
> And for thy truth.'

And that night, as he took a last look out over the thousand watch-fires of pilgrims from all lands, the great song of joy that all Jewish boys knew must have sprung to his lips:

> 'Many nations shall go up and say,
>   Come ye, and let us go to the mountain of the Lord,

And to the house of the God of Israel;
And he will teach us of his ways,
And we will walk in his paths.
For out of Zion shall go forth instruction,
And the word of the Lord from Jerusalem.'

Soon after sunrise next morning Jesus with Joseph started down the steep way from the Mount of Olives into the Kidron Valley. Across the valley Jerusalem was circled by her splendid walls. Crowned by a hundred towers, these battlements, built by Herod, ran for four miles round the city. On the east side, facing the Mount of Olives, no gate was open. How would they be able to enter the city and get into the Temple?

At the foot of the hill they crossed the rocky bed of the Kidron which was always dry except when the storms of winter raged. With the crowd of pilgrims they climbed more slowly the stone-stepped street built by the Romans up the hill Ophel on the south-east corner of the city outside the walls. They then turned right to the south wall of the city and passed through the shadow of one of its deep arched gateways. Jesus and Joseph moved through the jostling crowd in the narrow streets between the rows of little shops. In this one sat a leather-worker repairing a camel-saddle. There a pilgrim was buying dates and olives. Yonder sat a cheese-merchant weighing out his wares. Round the corner could be heard the hammering of the copper-smith. Some of the streets were called after the merchandise or craft of the men living in them; for instance, Wool Street, Cornmarket, and so on.

Jesus and his father had now come right round from the east to the west side of the Temple, where thousands of pilgrims were moving. At last Jesus set foot on the Tyropaeon bridge, fifty feet broad, with the great spring-stones of its arches, twenty-four feet in length. Looking down over the parapet he could see the valley two hundred and twenty feet below him. For this bridge led from Mount Zion, where Joseph and he had now climbed, to Mount Moriah, on which the Temple was built.

They crossed the bridge and pressed through the multitude under the great gateway into the outer court of the Temple. This majestic Court of the Gentiles (or the Nations) went right round the four sides of the Temple. As Jesus walked into the southern arcade of this court, he found himself in one of the most marvellous buildings in the world. A vast roof lined with cedar wood ran more than seven hundred feet in length. It was held up by a forest of Corinthian marble pillars, each a hundred feet high; and on either side were beautiful aisles with pillars fifty feet high. This was only one of the four colonnades that surrounded the Temple and that together formed the Court of the Nations.

The lowing of cattle, the bleating of thousands of lambs, the cooing of unnumbered doves, greeted the boy's ears as he walked into this court. Noisier still were the angry protests of the people arguing with the money-changers who often cheated the pilgrims from distant lands; as well as with the merchants to whom they went to buy a lamb or a dove for sacrificing in the Temple. The Law of Moses said that the doves and the lambs for the sacrifice must be without any spot or blemish. Those sold in the Temple Courts had been examined and passed by the priests as fit for sacrifice. Every family, coming up to the Feast, made it their very first act to sacrifice a dove or a lamb to God in the Temple to win forgiveness for their sins.

Joseph, therefore, bought a lamb and gathered it in his arms to carry to the altar of sacrifice. Joseph also now paid his Galilean shekel into the Temple treasury,[1] as every pilgrim, except women, children, and slaves, had to do before he could make his sacrifice.

[1] Equal to about one shilling and twopence.

Jesus and Joseph were still in the Court of the Gentiles. Now, however, they came to some steps leading up to another higher inner court. Alongside these steps Jesus saw this inscription in large Greek capital letters on the Stone of Forbidding:

> 'LET NO FOREIGNER ENTER WITHIN THE SCREEN AND ENCLOSURE AROUND THE HOLY PLACE. WHOEVER IS TAKEN SO DOING WILL HIMSELF BE THE CAUSE THAT DEATH OVERTAKES HIM.'

Joseph would indeed have been astonished if he had been told that the boy Jesus who walked that day up those steps with him, would one day declare to the world that God could be worshipped anywhere, as the Father of all nations, and that it was not His will that men should be killed for coming into any place to worship Him. Four shining gates of gold and silver faced Jesus as he stood on the terrace. Through one of these he and his father walked into the Court of the Women. It was so called because Jewish women could come into it, as well as men, though they could not pass through it nearer to the Altar of Sacrifice. From this court fifteen steps led up to the Court of the Men of Israel. At the top of these steps Jesus saw that wonder of the world, 'the Gate Beautiful', a towering maze of beautifully wrought Corinthian brass shining like gold. It was so massive that when it was opened in the morning and shut at sunset, it took twenty strong men to move it. Up those steps and through that gate a boy might not go. So, leaving Jesus there, Joseph walked up the steps and through the gate carrying his lamb. Men at the gate sounded blasts on trumpets. Joseph slew his lamb; the blood of the sacrifice was carried in a silver bowl to the altar. The parts of the lamb that must be kept for the Passover supper that night were placed on a dish and held up at the altar while incense was burned.

Joseph received back the parts of the Passover lamb and passed out.

Jesus, while waiting, heard the Levites at the top of the steps singing the psalms that praise God for the escape of the people of Israel from the slavery of Egypt.

Something far more arresting than even that held his attention. Under the cloisters, seated at the foot of a pillar, was a wise-looking rabbi. Around him stood a group of young men, pupils of his, listening to what he said. Now and then one of them asked him a question. Jesus, whose twelve-year-old mind was tingling with new ideas and unanswered questions, longed to stay and listen.

Joseph came out from the Court of the Men of Israel. Mary was waiting on the Mount of Olives. They hurried back to give to her the sacred parts of the lamb to be roasted for supper. When evening came and all was ready, a cup of red wine and water was poured out for each of those present. Then Jesus, as the youngest, poured water on the fingers of all, so that with clean hands they could begin the sacred feast. But before they started he asked, as the youngest always did at Passover: 'Why is this night different from all other nights?' and Joseph related the story of the escape of the Hebrews from Egypt.

Jesus' voice rang out with the others as they then sang the beginning of the 113th Psalm, crying:

> 'From the rising of the sun
> Unto the going down of the same
> The Lord's name is to be praised.
> The Lord is high above all nations,
> And his glory above the heavens.'

After another rinsing of hands, bitter herbs to remind them of the suffering of the slaves in Egypt were placed between slices of bread—unleavened bread to recall the haste with which the Israelites set out. This sandwich, dipped in a paste of fruits and vinegar, was eaten before the Passover Lamb and other dishes. Then, after a grace had been said, the second and longer part of the Hallel was chanted. Jesus sang with the others the closing psalm of this crowded day:

> 'I will pay my vows unto the Lord,
> Yea, in the presence of all his people,
> In the courts of the Lord's house,
> In the midst of thee, O Jerusalem.
> Praise ye the Lord.'

'Why is this night different from all other nights?'

For Jesus it was different in a way undreamed of by Joseph. A growing boy, he had come straight out of the home-life of Nazareth, where the stories of his people's history had filled him with thoughts of the coming of the Deliverer, the Messiah. He had walked with the pilgrims to the Temple to worship the Most High. Above everything in the world they longed for the coming of their Messiah. When will he come to save the people? they asked. How would that rabbi by the pillar among his pupils have answered that question? How would Jesus himself answer it? As he lay down that night he had a deeper idea than ever before of the longing of his scattered nation for the Messiah and of the greatness of the love of the Father for all His children. Desire burned in him to go again to the Temple Courts and there learn more of his Father's business.

In the morning there was the bustle of getting ready to go back to Nazareth. The Passover Supper had been celebrated; the Temple Sacrifice made. The Festival would last for days longer. Thousands stayed to learn from the rabbis, or to renew friendships. But Mary had the other children at home on her mind. Joseph could not forget the ploughs waiting to be repaired, the chests and doors and yokes on order from his neighbours in Nazareth. So they rolled up their simple travelling mats and with their fellow pilgrims from Nazareth started off. Joseph and Mary never doubted that Jesus was among them. The caravan trailed out along the north road from the end of the Mount of Olives. As the sun went down they had reached Beeroth, where the travellers to the north from Jerusalem usually camped.

As the clusters of relatives got together for supper, Joseph and Mary began to look for their boy. 'Have you seen Jesus?' they asked this neighbour and that. All replied that they had not got a glimpse of him all day. Joseph and Mary were greatly worried. What could have happened to him? Could he be lost in Jerusalem? But why should he stay? With whom could he be? What was he doing?

'We must turn back and search,' they agreed. But the sun had set. Joseph could not go back through the night with Mary on a road where robbers might set upon them. Nor would she go on with the caravan northward, wondering what might have come to her son. So they stayed the night there. But, as soon as the first glint of dawn tinged the sky, they were up and hastening back down the road to Jerusalem. That afternoon they spent going to one after another of the houses of acquaintances in Jerusalem and searching along the Mount of Olives; but all in vain.

On the third morning they recommenced their search with heavy hearts. They went into the still crowded Temple Courts. As well look for a needle in a haystack as for a boy among these thousands. Suddenly they saw him, his face tense with eagerness, a glow in his eyes. He was standing with others around a group of wise, kindly faced rabbis, asking and answering questions.

How came he to be there?

When he awoke on the morning after the Passover Supper, the shining thoughts that had thrilled his soul the day before filled his whole being. There, right before him across the valley, lay the Temple. How he longed to get there, to listen to the great teachers; to ask his eager questions; to say what was burning in his own heart! Away he went down the hill, up the other side, over the bridge, into the courts of the Temple. On the terrace he found the group that he sought. Drawing near he began to listen. By and by he asked a question. A rabbi, answering, put to the boy another question; and he joined in the discussion. Many things may have been talked about. One subject we can be sure was discussed, for it filled the minds of Jews everywhere. When will the promised Deliverer, spoken of by the prophets, come, bringing in the new age, the Day of the Lord? When will the Messiah come? What will he say and how will he act? What will be his character; and what will be the nature of his rule? Will he destroy the rule of Rome? Or will he bring simply the rule of justice and mercy? Or will he free men from the slavery of their sin, as a man could buy (or redeem, as Roman law put it) his slave into freedom and adopt him as a son?

Jesus even as a boy knew that God was a Father. If He was a Father and loved His children, then His Messiah must be like Him in being full of loving-kindness to all that He had made.

Jesus spoke of these things with the rabbis naturally and simply, as he would talk of his home and his mother and brothers and sisters. The hours passed quickly. All sense of time was lost. The shadows in the Temple lengthened. Somewhere, somehow, he slept and took food. The next day and the next still found him in quest of truth.

Suddenly, the voice that he knew best in all the world rang in his ears, full of sorrow and joy, reproach and gladness blended.

'Son,' said Mary, 'why have you dealt thus with us? Behold, your father and I have sought you sorrowing.'

He turned. Love and surprise were both in his eyes. 'How is it,' he asked in astonishment, 'that you sought me?

Did you not know that I must be about my Father's business?'

His mother could not understand what he meant by this. But she kept the saying, and all that had happened, in her heart and often thought over it.

Jesus knew, as he looked into his mother's face, that for him to be 'about my Father's business' meant to go home and, in the happy companionship of the home at Nazareth, to be subject to his parents. So, saying 'Good-bye' to his friends, he went with Joseph and Mary out from the Temple and took the road north over the hills to Nazareth.

CHAPTER IV

'MY FATHER'S BUSINESS'

WHEN Jesus walked over to his father's workshop on
the day after they reached Nazareth from Jerusalem,
the shops that he saw on the way; the plane, the mallet,
and the chisels, the planks, were all the same; but he now
saw with new eyes.

For years he had as a small boy skipped along the
narrow, steep Nazareth street with its little shops, and had
watched the leather-worker, the potter, the weaver, and
the others at their work, while the neighbours chatted
and bargained with them for sandals, water-jars, and cloaks.
These were then the only shops that he had ever seen. But
now, as a twelve-year-old boy, he had been in Jerusalem,
the great city. There he had watched the thousands of
pilgrims chaffering in the Temple Court, and in the
hundreds of booths. So the walls of his home town had,
as it were, opened for him, and he had a glimpse of the
wide, many-coloured world of men from east and west. He
had talked of the greatest things in life with the wisest
teachers of his world-scattered people. In his talks with
those rabbis in the courts of the Temple, Jesus found more
and more of the meaning of his own life. As the writer,
Luke, said, 'He grew in wisdom.'

Jesus had already begun to help Joseph at his work; for
some day the main support of the family would fall on his
shoulders. So he must learn the craft of carpenter, but
now that he had come back from Jerusalem, 'to be about
my Father's business' as a carpenter was now a greater
thing than he had dreamed. Jesus thought about all this
as he sat on the floor of the workshop, among the shavings
and sawdust, helping to hold a curved branch that Joseph
was shaping into a double plough-yoke for oxen.

Joseph, too, sat on the ground with his feet bare for most of his work. He gripped the wood not only with his hands, but with his feet. Jesus' muscles grew strong, his shoulders broadened, his chest deepened, and his fingers grew more powerful and skilful, as he learned to drive the saw, send the shavings flying from his plane, make a clean cut with his sharp chisel, and hammer home the wooden pegs in the tough beams of the frame of a new house.

As the neighbours came into the shop, Jesus saw that they asked Joseph to do many different pieces of work. This farmer wanted a yoke and a hoe-handle; that cloth-merchant needed strong shelves in his shop on which to show and store his wares; the grain-merchant up the street needed a corn-measure; while that father of a family wanted a chest to present to the bride and bridegroom at his daughter's wedding. As a town carpenter, Joseph, and Jesus after him, was also a house-builder and a cabinet-maker. A house would fall to pieces if he did not make a sturdy frame of strong supports and roof-beams, which were all cleverly morticed and held together by wooden pegs. He must know both how to choose the toughest wood and how to shape it well. The frame of the house must rest on good foundations, so that when the winter rains beat upon it and the winds howled down from the north against the walls, it should not fall into ruin.

The quick ears of the boy caught the gossip of the men who came into the workshop to order goods or to fetch them away. This farmer needed a new plough, since his had been broken by the small iron share striking a boulder when he was ploughing with an angry ox. He told of the thorns and thistles and poisonous darnel that choked his crops, the birds that snatched away the seed, and how the scorching sun burnt up the young barley where the soil was shallow. But what wonderful ears of corn, he added, grew on the crop that survived all these dangers—up to a hundred grains on an ear. The corn-merchant of Nazareth talked of the camel-caravans bearing grain from the rich uplands across Jordan. The camel-men had given him the gossip of Damascus and of Egypt, the places between which they travelled. So Joseph and Jesus heard the news of the wider world.

Some relatives of the Nazareth family lived beside the Lake of Galilee, only a day's walk distant over the hills. They were fishermen and sometimes walked up on to the Galilee highlands. They would call in at the workshop and give Joseph and Jesus the news of Capernaum with its busy market thronged with merchants from Persia, Greece, and Egypt, and even Rome. They told the events, too, of the many thriving towns on the lake shore where fish were salted to be carried to all parts of the Roman Empire. While these Galilee sailor-fishermen chatted in the workshop, a shepherd would come in from the hills, telling how the hyenas and wolves were growing more and more daring as they prowled around his sheep-fold. A good shepherd must be ready, Jesus realized, to lay down his life for his sheep.

At the close of each week's work, the sound of a trumpet rang through the streets. Every one began to move more quickly. The Hazzan, of the House of Gathering, the Synagogue, had climbed to the roof, and was warning Nazareth that in half an hour the Sabbath would begin.

In the next few minutes Jesus had put away the tools. Strapping on his sandals and shaking the shavings and sawdust from his tunic he walked home. Joseph went to the Synagogue. When the father returned, Mary and Jesus, with the other boys and girls, gathered at the doorway while Joseph prayed that the Sabbath would come like a bride into the house and take charge of it. He took a cup and holding it in his hands asked a blessing. He handed the cup to each of the family in turn. A small water-

The grain-merchant at Nazareth

pitcher was now brought by one of the younger children. Each held out his hands, while the running water was poured over the fingers. This was to cleanse the body— as the prayer had purified the spirit—in preparation for the Sabbath, which lasts from sunset to sunset.

In the early sunshine next morning, the family went towards the place of worship. They walked up the stone steps under the wide porch into the cool shade of the synagogue. They took their usual places, sitting on the floor on mats. In front was a platform. On it stood a broad reading-desk. Behind the platform a curtain hid a cupboard, called the Ark of the Sacred Scrolls. This was the most sacred part of the synagogue, for in it were the precious manuscript rolls of parchment on which all the Law and the Prophets were carefully written in beautiful script.

In some special seats facing the congregation sat old men and leaders of the Jews. These were the chief seats in the synagogue. In the centre of these sat the Ruler of the synagogue, called the Parnas. He chose the men who should read aloud to the people the paragraphs from the Law and the Prophets. Not far from him was the Shamas: he was the attendant and had many things to do, including keeping the building clean, filling the lamps with oil, and spreading sweet-smelling herbs on the floor.

Jesus saw that all his neighbours and friends were now settled quietly in their places. The service was about to begin. The Hazzan—he who had sounded the trumpet from the roof—sang:

> 'Holy, Holy, Holy, Lord God of Sabaoth.
> O give thanks unto the Lord
> For He is good.'

To this all the people sang in responsive chorus: 'For His mercy endureth for ever.'

Then all rose to their feet and together said the 'Hear, O Israel,' which was on the parchment on the doorpost on all their houses. After this, one of the seven men chosen by the Ruler of the Synagogue to read on that Sabbath, stepped forward. The Hazzan, pulling aside the curtain, opened the doors of the cupboard and drew out the Scroll for the day. Many of the people rose from their seats and pressed forward to show their reverence by kissing the parchment. One reading was from one of the books of the Law—Numbers, for example, or Deuteronomy, or Leviticus; another was from one of the prophets, perhaps the Scroll of Amos, or of Jonah, or of Isaiah, or of Micah.

When they had listened to the reading, and had sung and prayed, one of the rabbis from his chair spoke for a little time of the meaning of the words that they had read. The service was closed with a prayer, and all went home.

Thus the years passed, on week-days labouring with his hands, on the Sabbath attending the service of God, Jesus lived on for some eighteen years after his first visit to Jerusalem. During all those years the carpenter's shop, the street, the synagogue, the home, the hill-top, were the school in which he 'grew in wisdom and in stature and in favour with God and man'.

One day Joseph was not well enough to go to the work-shop. He grew worse and died. When Joseph was gone, Jesus' shoulders took the burden of the family of seven people.

CHAPTER V

THREE YOUNG MEN

'THE new Governor from Rome is sailing into the harbour,' shouted the boys of Caesarea Palestina to one another. They raced down to the harbour to see his ship come in and watch him land. Many of the boys were in time to see the great sail of the galley-ship-come down, and to watch the steersmen lean hard on the tiller-sweeps that jutted from the stern. The ship swung round the end of the gigantic mole that Herod the Great had built, and the oars of the galley-slaves slowly moved the boat towards the moorings.

Even a Roman, like the Procurator, as the governor was called, accustomed to great buildings, could not but be moved to wonder at this marvellous curved breakwater that stretched across the whole bay. It was half a mile long, and so broad that three chariots could be driven abreast along the top. Herod had brought skilled architects from Egypt to superintend the work, and many thousands of slaves to quarry from the mountains, drag to the beach and transport into the harbour, the huge stones of this pier. So he had changed a stormy open roadstead into one of the noblest and safest harbours in the world. Behind it he had built a palace-citadel and a marble theatre, and had created a new city. Caesarea Palestina was now the seat of the Roman government of the Province of Judaea; and all the city was agog to greet the new Procurator whom the Emperor Tiberius in Rome had appointed.

'Father says that his name is Pontius Pilatus,' cried one boy to another as they watched the stately ship come nearer to the harbour side. Pontius, his first name, came from an ancient Italian family that had won honour in the story of Rome. Pilatus, his second name, told of the pilatus or pike, the stout short spear used by the Roman legions that his fathers had led into battle. He must have had a third name, like other Romans, but we do not know what it was.

'There he is,' shouted the boys, pointing to a proud-looking man about thirty years old, who stood on the raised poop of the ship. By his side stood Claudia Procula, his wife, who was certainly wondering what her life would be like in this strange frontier land so far from the busy streets and gay society of Rome. The ship was moored, the gangway laid down, and amid the cheers of the people, the new Procurator and his wife came ashore to the castle that was to be their home for the next ten years.

Pilate was a young man to be made ruler of a province. Little Judaea, however, was one of the lesser procurator-ships given by the Emperor to ambitious young men. It was a terribly difficult country to govern. The Jews were restless and discontented; they hated to be subject to Rome; they clung to their old customs and religion, and broke into riot when these were interfered with.

About the time that Pilate came to take up the governor-ship, another young man, nearly Pilate's age, appeared on the scene.

John, some three months older than Jesus, was the son of a priest named Zacharias, who, every year, served in the Temple at Jerusalem. His wife was named Elizabeth, and their boy, John, was born in a town perched among the hills of Judaea. As a boy, John used to listen to his father and mother and their friends talking of the cruelty and misery and wrong that their land suffered and praying that God would send His Deliverer, the Messiah, to free them from their aggressors.

As he grew older, he looked out on the world. He saw the Roman rulers taxing the poor people; he saw also

Annas, the high priest, with his sons and his son-in-law, Caiaphas, growing rich on the dues exacted from the pilgrims to Jerusalem. The Romans, it was true, were harsh and cruel, but were there not great faults in his own people? Did they always love justice and mercy? Were they not sometimes greedy and grasping, more eager to be rich than to be good? What must be done to make things better?

Everybody would expect John to become a priest, like his father; for that meant a good wage and a position of honour and authority among the people. But John had other ideas. He felt that he must live apart from the busy world—get away to some quiet place where he might live a simple life. Putting on a rough tunic of camel-hair tied at the waist with a leather girdle, he left his home. Staff in hand, he plunged eastward into the wild desert to which the old prophets gave its true name—'Devastation.'

The brown sand and tawny limestone scorched his sandals. The sun's blazing heat was flung back by the rock of the bare hills. At night he lay on the hill-side with a stone under his head and watched the stars till he slept. At sunrise he climbed down into the valley where a solitary spring gave him drink. From a hole in a tree he scooped the honey of the wild bees. At times he was fed with roasted beans by some wandering Bedouin tribe.

There in his wild solitude John spent long hours in thought. He pondered on the unhappy lot of his people, and on the sayings of the prophets of old who foretold the coming of a Deliverer. When would that Deliverer come, he wondered. Surely it would be soon. But would the people be ready to receive him? Were they not too selfish, too much occupied in buying and selling, too forgetful of their duties to God and their neighbours? Must not their hearts be changed before the Deliverer could come among them? And by and by John came to believe that it was his mission in life to prepare the way for this Deliverer. He remembered the beautiful lines of the prophet Isaiah:

'The voice of one crying in the wilderness,
Make ye ready the way of the Lord,
Make his paths straight.
Every valley shall be filled,
And every mountain and hill shall be brought low,
And the crooked shall be made straight,
And the rough way smooth;
And all flesh shall see the salvation of God.'

John felt that he was the Voice. He must tell the people the thoughts that filled his own soul. Coming down from the hills to the banks of the Jordan, he stood at the cross roads by the ford. Men stopped to gaze at this young man, shaggy, lean, his face weather beaten and sunburnt, and to listen to the strange words that burst from his lips.

'Repent ye,' he cried, 'for the Kingdom of Heaven is at hand.'

Stories of the hermit were carried through the country-side. Peasants left their ploughs, merchants their accounts, labourers put down their tools, soldiers on leave came to hear him; even the tax-gatherers listened. So great was the sensation, so many were the people moved by John's message, that the very Sanhedrin in the Temple at Jerusalem, the Council of Sadducees and Pharisees, who ruled there, sent down a group to listen and report to them.

'Repent,' he cried.

'What must we do?' asked the people.

'If you have two coats,' he answered, 'give to the man who has none. Share your food in the same way.'

'What must we do?' asked a small company of tax-collectors.

'Do not collect more than the right taxes,' he retorted. The crowd smiled at this.

A group of soldiers edged towards John.

'And we,' they inquired, 'what must we do?'

'You must not seize people's goods by force. Do not bring false charges against them; but be content with your army pay.'

He thus told them all that, as preparation for the Rule of God, the Kingdom of Heaven, they needed to change, not their work, but their ways; be just and merciful and unselfish; a simple thing within the reach of every one, but difficult, for it called for a change of heart.

To all these working people he had spoken firmly but kindly. Suddenly, he swung round on the group of religious leaders who were listening, and addressed them sternly. He had seen the brushwood catch fire and the snakes writhing swiftly away to escape being burnt. He, who had in company with his father often visited the Temple, seized on this as a picture of these Pharisees and Sadducees from the Temple who had come down, not to hear his message and apply it to their own lives, but to criticize.

'You brood of vipers,' he exclaimed, 'who warned you to flee from the wrath to come? Bring forth fruits equal to your repentance. Do not say to yourselves: "We have Abraham for our father." I tell you that God can raise up children to Abraham out of these stones. Even now,' he cried, 'the axe is laid at the root of the tree. Every tree that does not bear good fruit is hewn down and used for firewood.'

By this he showed that they could not hope to be forgiven for wrong-doing in the belief that God specially favoured the Jews as descended from Abraham. To put away evil; to live a good life; that was the way into the Kingdom of God.

When a man said that he was sorry for his sins and wished to live a new life, John took him by the hand and plunged him into the running waters of the River Jordan. This represented the washing away of evil by the grace of God. It showed that they were of God's flock in the same way that a shepherd in the Jordan Valley who bought a sheep from another shepherd would plunge it into the river to cleanse it and to wash off the mark of its old owner.

The eager people, who had been waiting anxiously for the coming of the Messiah, began to whisper to one another—'This is the Christ.'

'No,' answered John when he heard this, 'I baptize you with water unto repentance: but he that cometh after me is mightier than I, whose sandals I am not worthy to bear: he shall baptize you with the Holy Spirit.'

It startled even Herod Antipas, the son of Herod the Great, who ruled over Galilee and much of the Jordan Valley. He feared a revolution and wondered whether it would not be wise to arrest John as a rebel.

The echo of John's trumpet-call came to Nazareth. It rang in Jesus' ears—'The Kingdom of God is at hand.' All the happenings of his life as a boy and a young man led up to this. The talks at home about the coming Messiah; the hours spent in the cloisters of the Temple as a twelve-year-old boy talking of the Kingdom of God; the words of the prophets in the Sacred Scrolls; all that he had ever thought and felt, told him that the time was come for him to be about his Father's business.

Jesus rose and told his mother and his brothers and sisters. The master-carpenter put away his tools. His Father's business was now something far bigger. James, Jude, and Simeon, now full-grown men, knew the whole craft of the carpenter, and could carry on the business and support their widowed mother. So Jesus walked out along the southern road into the Plain of Esdraelon. He never lived in his old home again. Hastening across the Plain he turned east into the Gap of Jezreel and took the paths down into the Jordan Valley. Reaching the ford where John was baptizing, he went to him and said:

'Will you baptize me?'

It may well be that John already knew Jesus. His piercing vision saw that Jesus had no need to repent of sins.

'No,' he replied. 'I need to be baptized by you; yet you come to me.'

'Come,' answered Jesus, 'this is how we should fulfil our duty to God.'

John took Jesus' hand, led him into the deeper waters, and baptized him. And then, as a dove gently settles upon her nest, so the Spirit of God came into Jesus' Soul. He heard the Voice of God saying: 'Thou art my Son, the Beloved, in thee is my delight.'

These words that came to Jesus as he stood by John in the Jordan were to lead him through strange adventures to the judgement court of the young governor, Pontius Pilate, who had just sailed into the port of Caesarea.

From the moment when, standing in the stream of the Jordan, Jesus heard the Voice say: 'Thou art my Son' all was new. He knew that he was God's Son, the Deliverer, the Messiah for whose coming the people longed. He had come to bring to the world the Good News that God was a loving Father, who cared for and watched over all his children.

The hum of the voices of the crowd on the banks and in the water buzzed about his ears. He must be alone. He must get beyond the range of the voices of men to listen to the clear, guiding Voice of the Father. He lifted his face to the hills. There was the wilderness. So Jesus turned west and striding along the river-side path climbed away from the stream up into a ravine leading to the heights. At last even the path failed. No human footsteps came that way. At sunset he was in a desert place of broken hills and boulder-strewn valleys where not a spring of water, not a house, not even a hermit's cave could be found.

In the darkness, 'he was alone with the wild beasts.' Prowling hyenas, howling jackals, passed down the valley in search of prey. With a stone under his head and no roof but the starry sky, Jesus' heart was full of joy. The Creator who made those stars loved him as His Son.

He, Jesus, was God's Messiah, the Christ. He had come into this desert-place to decide what that meant. What was he to do?

Thousands of young Jews were certain that the Messiah would ride at the head of armies, irresistible because God was with him; that he would drive the Roman rulers out of the land, and set up a new kingdom, with its throne in Jerusalem.

Every Jew knew by heart, as Jesus did, that passage written less than two hundred years before Jesus' birth, in which the writer of the Book of Daniel cried:

> 'I saw in the night visions,
> And behold, one like the Son of Man came
> With the clouds of heaven,
> And came to the Ancient of Days,
> And they brought him near before him,
> And there was given him a dominion,
> And glory and a kingdom,
> That all the peoples, nations and languages
> Should serve him:
> His dominion is an everlasting dominion,
> Which shall not pass away,
> And his kingdom that which shall not be destroyed.'

Those lively hopes of the coming of the Deliverer had been written in the days when the Syrian King, Antiochus Epiphanes, persecuted the Jews. But Judas the Maccabee had smitten the tyrant and set up a Jewish Kingdom. So the vision of the Son of Man had become gentler, and the writer of the Book of Enoch, a scroll that Jesus knew well, described him thus:

'A being whose countenance had the appearance of a man
And his face was full of graciousness, like one of the holy angels.

And I asked the angel who went with me and showed me all the
    hidden things,
Concerning that Son of Man, who he was, and whence he was . . .
And he answered and said unto me:
That is the Son of Man, who hath righteousness,
With whom dwelleth righteousness,
And who revealeth all the treasures of that which is hidden,
Because the Lord of Spirits hath chosen him.
And whose lot hath the pre-eminence before the Lord of Spirits in
    uprightness for ever.
And this Son of Man whom thou hast seen
Shall raise up the Kings and the mighty from their seats,
And shall loosen the reins of the strong,
And break the teeth of the sinners . . .
And the earth shall rejoice
And the righteous shall dwell upon it,
And the elect shall walk thereon.'

These were the pictures that Jesus knew of 'the Son of
Man' (the title that he took for his own.) More beautiful still
were two songs that had in them almost the very words that
God had spoken to him in Jordan. He had known them ever
since he was a boy. They must have come back to him as he
paced the Wilderness or sat under the night sky thinking:

'Behold my servant whom I uphold;
My chosen in whom my soul delighteth:
I have put my spirit upon him;
He shall bring forth judgement to the Nations.
He shall not cry, nor lift up,
Nor cause his voice to be heard in the street,
A bruised reed shall he not break,
And the smoking flax shall he not quench.
He shall bring forth judgement in truth.
He shall not fail nor be discouraged
Till he have set judgement in the earth;
And the isles shall wait for his law.'

'The Lord said unto me, "Thou art my Son,
This day have I begotten thee.
Ask of me, and I will give thee the Nations for thine inheritance.
And the uttermost parts of the earth for thy possession." '

These visions spoke of the Messiah as bringing in a new kingdom, a world-wide rule over many nations: or as judging the peoples. What kind of Kingdom should Jesus bring?

Without any protection from the heat of the sun except the shadow of some leaning rock, with no food or drink, Jesus waited there in the Wilderness. To the eagle quivering high in the air above him, to the passing wolf, he was just Man motionless, doing nothing. But in those forty days and forty nights he fought and won a battle in which the future of the world was at stake.

All the crafty skill of the Power of Evil was massed against him. The first attack was on his body. It was weak with the hunger and thirst of many days. He needed food terribly. With crafty cleverness and daring the Tempter took up the very words that God had spoken to Jesus in Jordan.

'If thou *art* the Son of God, command that these stones be made bread.'

What would be the harm in doing that? Just this, that it was his unique task to live in the Kingdom of God without using for his own good any miraculous powers; for only in that way could all men know that they too might follow him. Why had the Hebrews been hungry and thirsty in the desert? The words that Jesus had learned as a boy flashed into his mind:

'And God suffered thee to hunger . . . that he might make thee know that man doth not live by bread alone, but by every word that proceedeth out of the mouth of God.'

That was his reply to the Power of Evil; that man is above all things spirit: 'Man shall not live by bread alone, but by every word that comes from the mouth of God.'

So the Tempter fell back foiled in his first attack. But a still subtler attack was to be launched. Jesus had to face the question how he, the carpenter, was to become

The Wilderness of Temptation

the acknowledged Messiah, the Deliverer. With devilish ingenuity, the Tempting Voice took Jesus' own reply about living by the word of God, and himself quoted that word, suggesting a swift, daring deed that would bring the nation to his feet. This was the suggestion to mount the loftiest pinnacle of the Temple, the centre of the world-wide life of the Jewish nation, and throw himself down into the crowded temple courts, relying on the promise in the 91st psalm:

> 'He shall give his angels charge over thee.
> They shall bear thee up in their hands,
> Lest thou dash thy foot against a stone.'

If Jesus tested God's word in that way and if he was miraculously borne up, the whole nation would listen to him as sent from heaven. He could declare: 'I am the Christ'; for he would have proved by a thrilling display that God was on his side. Again the temptation came: 'If thou art the Son of God, cast thyself down.'

The words of God to Moses, spoken in Mount Sinai, and written in the same part of the same Scroll as those that Jesus had just quoted, came to him.

'Again,' he replied, 'it is written: "Thou shalt not tempt the Lord thy God" '—or, in modern language; 'You must not put the Lord your God through a test.'

Triumphant over this second temptation, Jesus, looking over to the eastern hills beyond Jordan, saw the western fringe of the lands that were the great empires of the East. The hills on which he stood were the eastern fringe of the greatest of all the world's empires that stretched across North Africa and Europe to the Atlantic Ocean. The empires of the world! One after another they had lorded it over his little nation. The Pharaohs of Egypt, the kings of Nineveh and Babylon, the tyrants of Persia and of Greece, and now Rome, mightiest of all. Jesus could be Emperor of the World.

In his ear the Voice whispered:

> 'To thee will I give all this authority,
> And the glory of them:
> For it hath been delivered unto me;
> And to whomsoever I will I give it.
> If thou therefore wilt worship before me,
> It shall all be thine.'

He had come to the fork in the road. If he refused, there was only one other way to set up God's Kingdom. It was by showing men the love and goodness of God and calling men to follow him. To do that would terribly disappoint the hopes of his nation.

Again Jesus fought and won his battle.

> 'Thou shalt worship the Lord thy God
> And him only shalt thou serve.'

The Messiah of God must be true to the character of God; so he must be love and mercy and goodness. Jesus' battles were won. For the time being, the Voice of the Tempter was silent. Jesus turned from the wilderness and went back among his own people to begin his work.

CHAPTER VI

NICODEMUS

JESUS had been alone with the wild beasts in the rocky wilderness of the hills of Judaea for nearly six weeks. He now walked quickly from the boulder-strewn hills to the rich soil of the Jordan Valley. He learned from passers-by that John was still at the ford surrounded by crowds come from all sides to listen to his words.

At last Jesus reached the river bank where the Voice of God, speaking in his soul, had said: 'Thou art my Son, the Beloved.' He waded across the ford of the Jordan and saw John. On the other side of the river was a village called Beth-abara, or the House of the Ford. There he found lodging, and stayed, listening to John, speaking with him, and mingling with the crowds of people.

Among these were many young men attracted by John's fiery spirit. Three of these had hurried thirty miles down the Jordan Valley from their homes on the northern shores of the Lake of Galilee, close to the place where the Jordan runs into it.

John the Baptist was standing one morning, on the day after the Sabbath, talking with two of these young men from Galilee who had been baptized by him. They were friends and often worked together fishing with their nets from their boats on the Lake. One of them had a Greek name, which was not usual in a Jew. He was called Andrew, which means 'manly'. He was born and lived in a village called Fisher-home, or Bethsaida. Andrew had a married brother named Simon, who lived in the neighbouring town of Capernaum. With Andrew was his young friend, John, who also lived at Bethsaida. John had a younger brother named James. They lived at home with their father, Zebedee, and their mother, Salome.

These young men were fired with the message of John the Baptist about the Kingdom of God and had become followers of his. As Andrew and John were talking with John the Baptist he suddenly pointed to a man coming down the river-bank.

'Look,' said John.

Turning, the two young fishermen saw a young, bearded, country workman wearing the ordinary clothes of a Galilean townsman, a tunic of home-spun wool, woven in one piece.

'Behold,' said John the Baptist, 'the Lamb of God.'

There was something in Jesus, they could not tell what, that attracted the young fishermen. Andrew and John left John the Baptist and walked along the bank following Jesus. Hearing them behind him, he turned and stopped.

'What do you want?' he asked.

Taken aback, they could only stammer out another question: 'Teacher, where are you staying?'

'Come and see,' was Jesus' invitation.

So the three men of Galilee walked along, side by side, until they reached the place where Jesus was lodging. They entered and the young men sat listening to Jesus while the hours slipped by. The sun set and they sat on the roof-top under the night sky, while Jesus told them of his vision of the Kingdom. It was the most wonderful adventure of their young lives. John, dictating his recollections half a century later, recalled the actual time of day when they met.

Andrew was so certain that here was the great leader for whom his nation waited that, early next morning, he hastened to find his brother.

'Simon,' he exclaimed, 'we have found him, the Christ; come along and see him.'

So Andrew brought Simon to introduce him to Jesus. As these two looked into each other's eyes for the first time,

Jesus, reading the young fisherman's sincerity and simplicity, exclaimed:

'So you are Simon, the son of John—your name is to be Cephas—the Rock.' (Peter, as we call him, from the Latin word for rock.)

The three young fishermen had now no wish in the world so great as to be with Jesus. He decided to go north again to his and their home-land of Galilee. They all said 'Goodbye' to the gaunt, stern, yet loving prophet; and started homeward. They never heard John's voice again.

Climbing the caravan route north-westward out of the hot, damp air of the Jordan Valley to the fresh breezes of the Plain of Esdraelon, the four companions talked together of the future. On the way they encountered another Bethsaida fisherman who, like Andrew, bore a Greek name. He was called Philip, 'Lover of Horses'. So they climbed up the hills from the Plain past Cana of Galilee over the sheep pastures of the highlands, until at last, through a deep ravine in the hills they suddenly saw, far below them, a gleam of blue. It was the north end of the Lake of Galilee —the home of all of them, except Jesus—and now the only home that he was to have for the rest of his days.

They were now on 'The Way of the Sea', a famous caravan track along which thousands of camels passed every year bearing silks and spices, dates and fish, rugs and pottery, swords and daggers from Persia through Damascus for Rome and Egypt, Greece and Spain.

This highway swung round the north end of the Lake of Galilee and up the ravine which they had now entered. The four men, walking by a brawling stream along which shepherds and goatherds led their flocks, descended into the shadows of the Valley of Doves, famous for the birds that were caught here in hundreds to take down to the Temple in Jerusalem, there to be sold for sacrifice at the Altar during the high feasts.

Robbers' caves were hollowed in the high cliffs of the ravine. John's father had often told him how, when he was a boy, he had seen Herod the Great's soldiers hunting the Galilean rebels over the hills. The rebels had taken refuge in the hill-side caves. He, furious at being balked, ordered his soldiers to make great cages in which they were let down over the cliff on to the ledges of the caves. Then they dashed from the cages into the caves, carrying trusses of straw, and they set the straw afire with torches and thus smoked the rebels out.

Suddenly, the rocky valley widened into the lovely 'Garden of the Princes', the Plain of Gennesaret—sheltered by the hills, six hundred feet below sea-level, with warm breezes, plentiful rains, and refreshing dews. So Jesus and his friends walked in the shade of walnut groves and olive trees, through vineyards, plantations of figs and dates, and peach orchards that bore fruit for over nine months of the year. They passed by the walls of a little town called Magdala, and, turning to the left, skirted the lake for a few miles. Here the beach was beautifully shaped in a number of curving bays.

At last Simon cried, 'Here is home,' as they came upon a little bay into which a Roman aqueduct carried hot waters that gushed from the hill-side farther back, were used for healing baths, and then ran into the Lake. These waters attracted the fish so that the village, Fisher-home, or Bethsaida, had grown up on that site. John ran down to the beach to greet his father, Zebedee, and his brother, at work at their nets, and then home to his mother, Salome. Philip and Andrew made off to their homes. Simon, with Jesus, went over the next low ridge to the larger town of Capernaum, which did a big trade with the camel caravans from north and east, and had its customs frontier. Simon hastened to his home, where his young wife and her mother awaited him. Into that home Jesus entered; and Capernaum became the centre to which he came back again and again from the journeys that he took with Simon and the other young men who gathered around him.

Simon, who could never stay still for long, soon had his drag-net over his shoulder and his throw-net in his hand and was on his way down to his boat moored in the little bay. He waded into the warm shallows with the throw-net in his right hand. It was shaped like a parachute with weights round the edge. Swinging it round his head, he flung it out across the water as far as the cord that he held would carry. It swung open as it twirled, fell into the sea, and as it sank, the weighted edges went swiftly to the bottom and came together, enclosing a small catch of fish which he now dragged towards him.

It was spring time. The time of the Passover Feast was near. Jesus decided to go to Jerusalem. For it was now time to give to the wider world the Good News of the Love of God, and to explain what the service of God meant. It was a strange thing to try to do, for the million Jewish pilgrims from all over the Roman world who came to the feast each year had been taught that men need do no more than obey the Law of Moses, and that the rabbis in the Temple, and the high priests and the Scribes of the Great Council, the Sanhedrin, could alone explain that law to ignorant people. How, then, could a north-country carpenter, talking with a guttural accent that showed he came from a part of the world that was laughed at for its roughness and its ignorance, bringing as his companions horny-handed young men with the smell of the fish in their tunics, expect to be listened to when he spoke of the Kingdom of God?

Jesus, however, called his followers to go with him to the Passover. They started out over the hills and joined the caravan track that he had taken as a twelve-year-old boy. Among the pilgrims on the road, and those that they found, after three days' hard walking, when they came to the crest of the Mount of Olives and into the city itself, were men and women and even boys from all over the Jewish world. One had been perhaps a student in Athens University; another had pored over the thousands of tablets that made the wonderful library in Alexandria on the coast of Africa; a tent-weaver had come from Tarsus in Asia Minor (one man, Saul, may well have been there); a dyer from the far-away table-lands of Persia on the east; a silversmith from Massilia on the banks of the Rhone; a trader from Rome, and a rabbi from Ephesus; all these might jostle with the group of companions from Galilee as they walked on an afternoon of the Feast in the Temple Courts.

Seated on the ground by one of the pillars under the great cedar roof, Jesus began talking quietly with his friends. Others stopped to listen. He talked of the thing for which the Jews longed more than any other: the coming of the Kingdom of God. But he spoke about the Reign of God as coming, not with uproar and revolution, but silently, as the seed grows to harvest; and secretly, from within the hearts of men, as the yeast leavens the bread.

Hard-headed merchants, quick-witted students, rough-handed but thoughtful shepherds and farmers, practical working-men: all these and many others were in the group of pilgrims who gathered round Jesus in the Temple Courts. They listened because of the beauty and truth of what he said. They listened, too, because he did not give as his authority for what he taught that Moses or this or that prophet said these things. The very spirit of God was speaking in and through him.

Quickly some one went with the news to the white-bearded Annas, who had for years been high priest, and to his son-in-law, Caiaphas, who was high priest at this time.

'There is a new teacher,' they told Annas, 'talking in the

Temple Courts; a man from Galilee. Crowds are gathering to hear what he has to say. He says that the Kingdom of God is at hand.'

Annas was at once all ears. He scented danger to his power and his treasure-chest. He and five of his sons had been made high priests one after the other. Now his son-in-law, Caiaphas, held that post. Altogether, Annas and his family had become enormously rich by exacting large payments from the millions of pilgrims to the Temple. Again and again rebel leaders in Galilee—with the war-cry, 'the Kingdom of God'—had stirred the anger of Rome against Jewish nationalism and had even threatened the lordship of the high priests. Annas set to work at once to find out whether Jesus was dangerous or not.

Caiaphas was chairman of the Great Council in the Temple that ruled the religious life of the Jews. It was called the Sanhedrin and consisted of seventy-one members. They were divided into two sets who were violent opponents in most things, but always acted together if any one attacked the power of the Sanhedrin. One of these parties was called the Sadducees. There were not many of them; but they were rich, lived in palaces and great villas with crowds of servants. They were cold-blooded, proud, and hard-hearted; and looked down on the lower orders of the Temple priests. The High Priest was always a Sadducee. Annas and Caiaphas were Sadducees. They said that men's souls do not live for ever; that there are no angels or spirits; nor is there any judgement of man or resurrection. These were the men who, as we shall see, brought about the death of Jesus.

The other party in the Sanhedrin were the Pharisees. They were keenly religious; they believed that man has an immortal soul, will rise again and be judged by God, who is served by messenger-spirits, angels as we say. They looked for the coming of the Kingdom of God. Their idea, however, was that it would arrive when men obeyed absolutely, not only the Law of Moses, but the customs and rules which had been handed down through generations of their ruling men.

So the Sadducees and the Pharisees were constantly at odds, but they united in face of a danger that threatened them both. They were sure that they saw danger in Jesus. Here was a poor man, who had never had a rabbi's Temple education, a man who talked with a countrified accent, and whose hard hands were more used to a saw and a hammer than to a scribe's stylus and wax tablets, coming from that haunt of rebels, the highlands of Galilee, and teaching wild doctrine about the Kingdom of God.

There was one man among the seventy-one, however, who had a curious feeling that, after all, Jesus might be right. His name was Nicodemus. He had much money, was a deep scholar, very religious, and people paid great respect to him. But, in spite of all that, Nicodemus was not happy: he did not even feel at peace in his own heart. His wealth and learning, and even his religion, did not seem quite real to him. He walked quietly to where Jesus was talking and listened to him; looked at him. In Jesus' words and in his eyes, Nicodemus could see that this teacher had what he himself lacked; the most priceless gift in the world, strength of spirit and peace in his heart. And he could see, too, that to Jesus the Kingdom of God was real, here and now. Nicodemus asked himself how he could have this great gift? The only way was to go to Jesus and ask him.

How the Sanhedrin would jeer at Nicodemus if he told them what he was planning to do! He dared not face their scorn. He found out where Jesus was lodging in Jerusalem.

One night, when it was quite dark and the crowds had gone from the streets, Nicodemus wrapped his cloak around him and, with his face covered, made his way through the narrow streets of Jerusalem. Perhaps John led him up the stone steps outside the house to the flat roof where Jesus sat, and then himself sat where he could listen.

Nicodemus' first word was surprising. He was a learned member of the Sanhedrin and Jesus an unknown craftsman from the crude north. It showed, therefore, how great a hold Jesus' words had taken on him that he began with the word, 'Rabbi.'

'Rabbi,' he said, 'we know that thou art a teacher come from God.'

He was going on to speak of the things that Jesus did, but he was too timid to ask the question that was troubling him. Jesus, piercing at once to Nicodemus' need, said, 'Verily, verily, I say unto thee, except a man be born from above, he cannot see the Kingdom of God.'

Nicodemus was baffled.

'How can a man be born when he is old?' he asked.

He was not, of course, so stupid as to imagine that Jesus meant that a grown man must become a baby again. But like all Jews, he believed that the Kingdom of God was to be a Kingdom in this usual sense—that the Jews would be ruled, not by the Roman emperor, but by the Messiah on David's throne in Jerusalem. He did not understand that Jesus meant something quite different: that he was not thinking of an earthly kingdom at all. When Jesus said that a man must be born again he meant that his aims, his whole life, must be as completely changed as if he were a new creature.

Jesus went on to explain to Nicodemus.

'What is born of the flesh is flesh,' he said, 'and what is born of the spirit is spirit. Marvel not that I said unto thee, "Ye must be born from above." The wind bloweth where it listeth and thou hearest the voice thereof, but knowest not whence it cometh and whither it goeth: so is every one that is born of the Spirit.'

Nicodemus, still puzzled, said 'How can these things be?'

'Art thou a teacher in Israel,' asked Jesus, 'and knowest not these things? Verily, verily, I say unto thee, we speak that we do know, and bear witness of that we have seen.'

So the talk went on into the night; Jesus spoke to Nicodemus of how he himself was born from above and said that God had sent him to show men the way to the Kingdom.

'For God so loved the world,' the writer adds, 'that he gave his only-begotten Son, that whosoever believeth on him should not perish, but have eternal life.'

When the talk was over, Nicodemus took leave of Jesus and went back along the dark narrow streets to his rich home. He understood very little of what Jesus had said to him, but he felt that there was something wonderfully beautiful about this new teaching, something finer than anything he had heard before, and in his heart he was ready to follow the new teacher. But he never had the courage to say so publicly. He knew that if he did so he would be turned out of the Sanhedrin, and lose his position in Jerusalem society. Twice, however, as the story will show us, he revealed that he was at heart a follower of Jesus.

CHAPTER VII

A WELL OF WATER

THE Passover Feast was ended. The pilgrims went streaming homeward along the roads north, south, east, and west. Herod Antipas, in great state, marched his cavalcade proudly down the steep way from Jerusalem to the Jordan and, crossing it, was carried up the hill-sides and then up the dizzy cliffs on which his father had built the mighty castle of Machaerus. In this stronghold he could scoff at all comers: yet he was troubled in his mind. He had deeply insulted the Arab sheikh Aretas, and Aretas was getting his men together against him. They could never capture Machaerus Castle; but neither could Herod crush Aretas, for the Arabs simply vanished like the mist if he attacked them, and then they appeared again. What troubled Herod was that the Emperor of Rome held him responsible for the peace of the land; and all was unrest and rebellion.

Worse still, there was this agitating hermit by Jordan, raving about a new Kingdom. The man was probably mad, but he was dangerous. He might stir up a rebellion. Herod was powerless against Aretas; but he could silence John, who had been insolent enough to rebuke him for marrying his brother's wife. So he ordered John's arrest. A company of soldiers hurried from the castle up the Jordan Valley, where John was teaching at a place called Aenone. John was led in chains to the dungeons of Machaerus. The brave voice was silenced. Herod was sure that he would hear no more of the new Kingdom. The news of John's arrest spread quickly. Jesus heard it. Turning his face northward he led his disciples straight towards Herod's territory. He went forward immediately to take up the work that John could now no longer do. He, in defiance of Herod, went to proclaim on the shores of the Lake of Galilee in the ears of the people the same message that John had proclaimed on the banks of the Jordan: 'Repent; for the Kingdom of God is at hand.'

On the way northward Jesus and his men came down from the Judaean hills into the Plain of Cornfields, where the spring crops were fast ripening. In front of them was the stone mouth of the ancient Well of Jacob which Jesus had seen when he came that way as a twelve-year-old boy. The afternoon was drawing on. The disciples hurried ahead to the town of Sychar, less than half a mile distant, to buy food for their evening meal. Jesus sat down to rest by the well under the shade of the trees. He was close to the Roman road from east to west, which crossed not far away the ancient pilgrim and merchant track that he and his men were following from south to north.

As Jesus sat resting, a woman came towards the well, carrying her water-jar. When she came near, he smiled and said: 'Peace be with thee,' and then, 'Give me to drink.'

It was a simple request, but it filled her with astonishment. However, she tied the long cord to her jar and let it carefully down into the deep well.

'How is it,' she asked as she pulled it up and poured out some of the cool, fresh water for him to drink, 'that you— a Jew—ask me—a Samaritan woman—for water?'

Her astonishment was natural. Jesus had broken two great barriers that she had never seen broken. The first barrier was that the Jews and Samaritans detested and despised each other.

'When we were in exile in Babylon,' the Jews accused the Samaritans, 'you wedded Assyrian wives; and when foreign people came into Israel your fathers married them; and even worshipped the false gods of these barbarian women. So you are a mongrel people. You have defied and broken the Law of Moses.'

The Samaritans had offered in the old days to help the Jews in rebuilding the Temple at Jerusalem; but the Jews had refused contemptuously, declaring that the very touch of Samaritan hands would defile the stones of the Holy Place. The enraged Samaritans built a Temple of their own on the crest of Mount Gerizim, which Jesus could see as he sat by the well. They declared that there alone could the true God be rightly worshipped. Each side hurled at the other the vilest insults they could think of. Often these curses led to blows and many fights took place. Small wonder, then, that the Samaritan woman was startled when she heard a Jew not only speak kindly to her, but ask for a drink of water at her hands.

What astonished her still more was that a man should speak to her, a woman, in a public place. A Jew could not, in those days, speak in the street even to a woman with whom he was acquainted. To talk with a woman whom he had never seen before was thought unbecoming.

Jesus simply swept this aside, as well as the hatred of Jews and Samaritans; he was a man and she a woman; but both were children of the one Father.

The woman was to be still further amazed.

'If you had known,' Jesus went on, 'who it is that said "Give me to drink", you would have asked him and he would have given you "living water".'

The woman could not understand. Something in Jesus commanded her respect: yet what he said seemed impossible.

'You have no jar to draw with,' she cried, 'and the well is deep,' which was certainly true, for it was then over eighty feet deep. 'Are you,' she asked with a touch of scorn, 'greater than our forefather Jacob, who gave us this well and himself drank from it, he and his sons, his flocks and his herds?'

'Whosoever,' replied Jesus quietly, 'drinketh of this

water will thirst again, but whosoever drinketh of the water that I shall give him will never thirst. The water that I shall give him will become a spring of water within him, welling up into everlasting life.'

Did the woman understand the truth of his words?

'Sir,' she said, 'give me that water, so that I may never thirst, nor come continually all this way to draw water from the well.'

Her words 'all this way' must have been spoken with a sigh; for she had to walk half a mile each way as often as she needed more water. It seems at first strange that she did not draw her water from the spring at Sychar, at the bottom of Mount Ebal, close by her home. There are three reasons that could draw her to the well. It was Jacob's well: 'our father, Jacob' she called him with pride. Secondly, the water is far sweeter than that at Sychar, and it is renowned for its purity and health-giving power. The third reason was hidden. Jesus revealed it through a sudden demand which startled her more than all that had gone before.

'Go,' he said, 'call your husband and come back.'

'I have no husband,' she replied.

'You speak truly,' Jesus answered; 'you have no husband: for you have had five husbands and the man you have now is not your husband.'

This was the third reason for her coming to the well. For her way of life would bring on her the anger of the women of Sychar; and the Sychar water-spring was the great meeting-place of the town's womenfolk. Naturally, she avoided it.

'Sir,' she exclaimed, 'I see that you are a prophet.'

Then she tried to change the subject.

'Our ancestors worshipped on this mountain,' she said, pointing to the Temple on Mount Gerizim, 'but you Jews say that men must worship in Jerusalem.'

This speech drew from Jesus words that stand among the greatest that ever fell from his lips.

'Believe me, O woman, the time is at hand when men will worship God neither in this mountain, nor in Jerusalem. The time is at hand, nay it now is, when the true worshippers will worship the Father in spirit and in truth, for indeed the Father desires such worshippers. God is spirit; and they that worship him must worship in spirit and in truth.'

The woman could no longer mock at Jesus. She quietly replied: 'I know that the Christ is coming; when he is come he will tell us everything.'

So it came about that a despised Samaritan and a woman was the first to hear from Jesus the truth that he was to hide for long months from the leaders of his nation.

'I who now talk with you am he.'

The disciples had now returned. They looked askance at this Samaritan woman talking with their master. Catching their frowning glances, she hurried away. She was all agog with her marvellous news; so excited that she left her jar as she fled down the road.

'Come,' she called to the men of Sychar, 'and see a man who has told me everything that I have ever done. Can this, think you, be the Christ?'

The disciples, still upset that their master had been talking with her, nevertheless did not dare question him. Instead they laid out their purchases at the well-side, and, knowing that he had had the long day's walk, cried: 'Rabbi, eat of this food.'

'I have food to eat of which you know nothing,' he answered.

'Can it be,' they asked one another, 'that some one has brought food to him?'

'My food,' Jesus pursued, 'is to do the will of Him that sent me and to achieve His work.' Then, pointing at once to the cornfields and to the men who were now hurrying down the way from Sychar towards Jesus, he exclaimed:

'You say, "It still wants four months to harvest." But behold, I say unto you, the fields are already white unto harvest.'

'The proverb "One sows and another reaps," is true', he added, 'I send you to reap a harvest for which you have not sown, other men have sown and you reap.'

The Samaritans, stirred by what the woman had told them about Jesus and eager to see if, indeed, the Messiah had come, pressed near to Jesus.

'Stay with us at Sychar,' they urged him; which was a wonderful thing for Samaritans to ask of a Jew. Jesus accepted their invitation. As he and his disciples walked with them up the way to the town, they beset him and John, Andrew, and Simon, with questions. He stayed with them for two full days and they sat eagerly around him listening to the Good News of the Kingdom of God, the Rule of the Father in the lives of His children. By the time Jesus said 'Good-bye' to them, many were sure that he was indeed the Christ; and believing in him, they became his followers. They said to the woman: 'We no longer believe because you said it: we have heard for ourselves and we know that in truth he is the Christ.'

Jesus and his men again took the northern trail homeward. For a long spring day they walked through the pleasant valleys of Samaria, where the sunlight glances on the tiny rivulets tinkling down the channels which had been hewn in the rock or dug in the rich soil by the farmers to carry the water from the hill-springs to the roots of their vines and almond trees. The rising sun saw them walking in the shadows between Mount Gerizim and Mount Ebal at the southern gateway of Samaria; in the late afternoon they could rest where the last curving hills of northern

Samaria drop to the edge of the Plain of Esdraelon,[1] and gaze on the Galilean hills outlined against the setting sun. Among those hills was home.

All next day they walked across the Plain by the field-paths through the late spring crops of barley until towards evening they crested a hill that looked down into the sunny village of Cana.

Pilgrims going northward from Jerusalem had got home days ahead of them, while Jesus was teaching in Samaria. They had spread the news of Jesus' work among the pilgrims in Jerusalem; and that he was on the way back to Galilee.

This news reached the eager ears of one of Herod Antipas' state officials. He may well have been one of the staff of Herod's Steward, Chuza. His boy lay ill, so ill that he was dying. The doctors had done all that they could; but now threw up their hands in despair as the boy tossed in the delirium of high fever. The father, seizing on the slightest chance of Jesus being able to help him, mounted his horse and hurried up the boulder-strewn ravine of the Way of the Sea. For fifteen miles he rode through the heat of the day along that troublesome climbing path and over the rolling highlands of Galilee. It was seven o'clock in the evening before he found where Jesus was and reached Cana. The anxious father sped toward him and, leaping from his horse, implored Jesus to hurry back with him down to Capernaum.

'You people,' Jesus said with a view to discovering the man's faith, 'will not believe unless you see signs and wonders.'

The father, burning with anxiety, cried: 'Sir, come down before my son dies.' Jesus' heart leapt in sympathy with the man. 'Go home,' he said, looking the father straight in the eye; 'your son lives.'

[1] See map.

Before dawn the man was on the road homeward. About half-way he saw some of his own staff of servants hurrying toward him, waving their arms and laughing with joy. As soon as they were within earshot they cried out:

'The boy is healed.'

'At what hour was he healed?' asked the happy father.

'At seven o'clock yesterday evening,' they replied.

With a light heart the father went on his way home to Capernaum. His wife greeted him and they rejoiced together. All his family believed in Jesus and became disciples of his, and helped to swell the warm welcome that greeted him when he came that evening into their city.

Next day Simon took his throw-net and went down to the beach. Wading in, he began to fish where the Seven Springs pour their healing waters into the Lake. Andrew, his brother, was with him.

Some distance away by the same beach a boat lay rocking. In it sat a fisherman, named Zebedee, and his two sons John and James. John had been talking with his father about his experiences in Jerusalem and Samaria in Jesus' company. His admiration of Jesus glowed in all that he told his father and brother, as they all worked together repairing with tough thread the fine nets with which they had been fishing in the night.

For Simon and Andrew and James and John life could offer no adventure more splendid than to go into the world with Jesus; to see his mastery as he changed the world for the tormented father by healing his son; to hear from his lips the truth that lighted up the whole of life like sunshine gleaming on the Lake; to learn, as they watched him talking with the woman, that courtesy and purity and loving-kindness are the brothers of courage and of strength. Even as Simon and Andrew were thinking of him, they heard his voice calling to them from the shore. He had made a great decision. John the Baptist was imprisoned in Herod's castle. His voice was silent. Herod might any day seize Jesus himself. But the Kingdom of God must be proclaimed, and men's bodies and souls made fit for it. The only way to make it impossible for any tyrant to prevent the new teaching from spreading was to light the fire, so to speak, in the minds of a group of young friends. So Jesus decided to call these young disciples of John the Baptist who had been with him at Jerusalem, and to keep them always with him. It was to do this that he came down to the beach that morning.

'Follow me,' he called to Simon and Andrew who were standing waist-deep in the lake ready to throw their nets. 'I will make you fishers of men.'

They instantly flung their nets over their shoulders, waded ashore and walked with Jesus along the beach. There they came to the boat in which Zebedee was at work with James and John. Again Jesus said:

'Come and follow me. I will make you fishers of men.'

The youths were over the edge of the boat in an instant.

So these four men set the sails of their young lives to the wind of the spirit that 'bloweth where it listeth', and put the tiller into Jesus' hands, so that he should guide their ship into stormy or quiet waters as he willed, and give them the word to let down the net as Fishers of Men.

CHAPTER VIII

'ALL THE CITY AT MY DOOR'

WITH his four friends Jesus walked on the Sabbath through the narrow streets of Capernaum and climbed the broad steps to the portico of the synagogue.

Strict Jews from Jerusalem were horrified at the eagles and lions and other strange beasts carved on many of the richly ornamented stones of this building. This did not worry the Galilean Jews, who were always scandalizing the Temple rulers by their wild, rebellious ways. A rich Roman officer, commander of a 'century' of soldiers, had just built this magnificent building for their worship. Why should they worry if his architect and masons had put in a few carved animals among the carvings of Solomon's Seal, the Shield of David, and the bunch of grapes carried back by the men sent out by Joshua to spy out the land?

Like every other good Jew, Jesus went every Sabbath to the synagogue. This week, however, his worship there was to be a thrilling adventure, beginning a new life for him and his men.

The story of Jesus' doings in Jerusalem, and the marvel of the healing of Herod's officer's son, had made a great stir. So, naturally, when the Scroll of the Prophets had been read, the leader of the synagogue asked Jesus to speak to the people. Every eye was on him as he spoke. This was not only through curiosity, quickened by the wonders that had been done by this Nazareth carpenter. There was something so strong in the look of his eyes, so fearless in his words. They felt that God was speaking in him.

There was suddenly a piercing shriek. The people leapt to their feet.

'Art thou come to destroy us?' yelled the voice of a

The steps to the front portico and part of the west wall of the Synagogue at Capernaum

frenzied man. 'I know you who you are—the holy one of God. What have we to do with you, Jesus of Nazareth?'

All eyes were on the twisted face of the demon-haunted man, as he cried out to Jesus: 'Art thou come to destroy us?' Then they swung round towards Jesus to see what he would do. He looked straight into the eyes of the man: remorseless to the evil spirit that possessed him; loving to the soul of the man himself. Then Jesus' voice rang out with a thrilling strength and command.

'Come out of him,' he ordered. 'Hold your peace and come out of him.'

The man staggered. He fell full length on the floor. He gave a fearful shriek. In the silence that followed every one held his breath. The man rose quietly to his feet. He looked round with the happy eyes of a man at peace within himself. An excited clamour broke out.

'What is this new teaching?' cried one.

'He gave orders to the evil spirit!' exclaimed another.

'Yes,' ejaculated a third, 'and it came out of him.'

'The man is himself again,' they all agreed.

The amazed congregation broke up, and began to spread the news through the town. No one talked of anything else. As men went out of the town through the field-paths to the villages in the hills, or sailed over the Lake to the other towns on its shores, they told how this man from Nazareth, just over the hills, had cast a demon out of the possessed man.

Jesus, meanwhile, had gone to Simon's home with his friends. Simon's young wife was anxious. Her mother lay sick of a fever. Simon's impulsive heart leapt at once to the thought that, if Jesus could cast out the demon, he might cast out the fever. Sure enough, turning to where the woman lay on her mat on the floor, Jesus grasped her fevered hand. As he did so the fever left her and she felt quite strong again.

No sooner was she on her feet than she began to busy herself with making a meal ready. The day wore on. At sunset, as the Sabbath ended, the clatter of many footsteps and the murmur of a crowd arose. Simon, gazing from the porch of his house, was amazed to see the whole roadway full of people. 'All the city was at my door,' he used to tell his friends later. Some were limping on crutches; others were carried on litters; others cried or howled, the victims of the nerve-diseases so common in the damp heats of that deep valley.

Jesus went out into that crowd of the sick. With the authority of a man in whom the spirit of God dwelt, he went from one to another. The throng pressed round him, all eager to be helped and cured. He laid his hands upon boys shivering with fever and left them well and happy; he gripped hold of men shaking with palsy, spoke to women drained of their strength, stooped over little children at the door of death; and wherever he passed disease sank back defeated and health sprang into victory.

When at last the people had all gone home, Jesus turned with his followers into Simon's house. Full of wonder at the works of his master as Simon was, nevertheless, he was so tired that he dropped into deep sleep. Jesus lay near him silent, but awake. It was important for him to see clearly what he was to do next. Looking back over the day, he recalled that that morning in the synagogue he began the day by teaching the people the Good News of the Kingdom of God. The scream of the possessed man had caused him to stop his teaching and to heal. Since that moment he had not spoken a word of his message. All his time and strength had been absorbed in healing. That healing had already made him famous as far as swift feet and eager tongues could carry the story. Capernaum, where the caravan routes separated to Egypt and Persia, Rome and Athens, was a place where the Roman centurion, the Greek merchant, the Jewish rabbi or fisherman or farmer met. It was a centre from which the power of Jesus, his teaching and his healing, could spread. He had come to bring to the world the knowledge of the Rule of God and to win men to love and obey Him. But if he went on—as he had done that day—giving all his strength to the healing of men, he would have neither time nor strength to deliver his message.

What was to be done? Thousands were gathering from all sides to be healed. But the future of mankind depended on the spread of the Kingdom. To see what he ought to do, he needed to be quiet and alone. So Jesus rose silently a great while before day. He unlatched the door and strode along the street out of Capernaum, along the field-path and into the hills. There on the hill-top under the stars, the Lake below gleaming in the moonlight, he prayed to his Father.

By the time dawn broke over the Gadara hills beyond the Lake, his decision was made. He had just called Simon and Andrew, James and John from their fishing to make them fishers of men. He must train them for the work.

Simon woke with a start of dismay, to find that Jesus had vanished from his house, leaving no trace. In the street sick folk already clamoured for healing. Calling to Andrew and seeking out John and James, Simon set out to find Jesus and bring him to these people. The group at length found him on the hill behind the town, and exclaimed:

'All men seek for thee.'

To their dismay he said that he would not go to them.

'Let us go into the next towns,' he replied, 'that I may preach there also, for therefore came I forth.'

So the little group went along the winding tracks from town to town and village to village. Up on the higher hills behind Capernaum was a small city called Chorazin. Here Jesus found another synagogue, not so massive or

rich as that in Capernaum, but built overlooking the Lake
far beneath them. The custom of the Jews calls them to
their synagogues on the second and the fifth day of the
week, as well as on the last day—the Sabbath. The leaders
in the synagogue here and everywhere through all that
crowded hill-city of Galilee asked Jesus to speak to the
congregations. For his fame was gone through the land
and all wished to hear and see him. Many also wished to
be healed. So he went from place to place healing and
teaching. Even more important was it that, as he and his
disciples walked from one town to another, he should
answer their questions and open up to them the knowledge
of what the Kingdom of God is like. Jesus himself meant
to them more than anything that he said. Often they were
perplexed by his teaching, simple though it was. But the
strength and the courage that they saw in him, the never-
failing kindness, the strong faith in the goodness and the
love, the power and the wisdom of God, who was, he told
them, their Father—all this was like the clear sunshine in
the sky—light and warmth and strength to them.

The men and women as well as the boys and girls in the
synagogues at Chorazin and the other towns were surprised
at his teaching. They were startled, not because it was
difficult to understand, but because it was so simple and
new and so obviously true; and because he taught them
truth straight from God, not quoting what the rabbis had
said—the numerous rules known as 'The Tradition of the
Elders'. The Pharisees declared that a man could not be
saved unless he obeyed all these traditions. Poor people
could not possibly do this; they could not even learn them
all, much less carry them out. So even the kind-hearted
scholar, Rabbi Hillel, the greatest of all the Temple
teachers in Jesus' time, said: 'No peasant can be a sin-fearer,
and the people of the soil cannot be good.' What he said
was true, if to be good meant to obey all these thousands

of tiny rules, which even said, for instance, that if you walk on the grass you break the Sabbath, as that is a kind of threshing, and if you push the earth with your sandal that is Sabbath breaking, as it is a sort of ploughing. How startled, then, were the people when they heard Jesus attacking some of the rules. He said, for instance:

'Ye have heard that it hath been said: "An eye for an eye and a tooth for a tooth." But I say unto you: "That ye resist not evil: but whosoever shall smite thee on the right cheek, turn to him the other also. And if any man will sue thee at the law, and take away thy coat, let him have thy cloak also. And whosoever shall compel thee to go a mile, go with him twain. Give to him that asketh thee, and from him that would borrow of thee, turn not thou away."'

That teaching was easy to understand. It called to a man to be brave if he was to follow it out. Jesus taught these truths, not as though they were strange, but as though they were simple. This was because, in his thought and his life, everything flowed straight from God. If the nature of God is love, then we must do all that love tells us. Often he spoke of the nature of God as the reason for doing what he taught; as, for instance, in the most famous of his words:

'Ye have heard that it hath been said: "Thou shalt love thy neighbour, and hate thine enemy." But I say unto you: "Love your enemies, bless them that curse you, do good to them that hate you, and pray for them which despitefully use you, and persecute you; that ye may be the children of your Father which is in heaven: for he maketh his sun to rise on the evil, and on the good, and sendeth rain on the just and on the unjust."'

The Tradition of the Elders made men think of God as a hard judge secretly spying to find if they were obeying hundreds of petty rules. Jesus showed God to them as a Father who loves to give good gifts to his children; who creates all beauty and gives flowers more gorgeous colours than the robes of King Solomon; and calls his sons—not to a cold obedience to rules with the aim of winning salvation—but to attempt heights of daring and sacrifice for love's sake.

The world of disease and the fear of it in which men were chained was a dungeon haunted by the terror of evil spirits. As Jesus came to sick people the power of God in him called out the faith in them, and sickness and madness and death fled before health and reason and life. As a child troubled by an evil dream thrills with joyful relief to wake to sunshine and the laughter of his parents, so the people of Galilee, stricken by disease or in the grip of sin, rejoiced in the clear shining of the love of God that they found in Jesus.

'The Kingdom of God is at hand', he proclaimed. Close by; no—nearer still, within you! Nor did it need words to explain the Kingdom; it was in Jesus; it flowed from him like living water from the mountain side.

So Jesus went through Galilee. There were the busy fishing cities and Taricheae with its famous boat-building yards, and the still more famous salting sheds. There were hundreds of villages among the hills where the peasant-farmers tilled the vines and the fig-trees, and tended their sheep and their herds of goats, or went into the harvest field with their sickles.

At last, on a certain day, just outside a town, a man approached Jesus. The man was in despair and very wretched. On account of a dreadful disease he was not allowed to come near anybody, nor even to go into a village. To live a slow death, seeing everybody shun him, unable to talk with brother or sister, mother or father, wife or son, this was agony. As the man looked at Jesus a new hope arose in his heart. He had heard how Jesus healed many diseases. What if he could heal him of his leprosy, as we call it? Now that he saw Jesus coming along the path from the village, he knew that he could heal him. Running towards him, the man flung himself on his knees:

'If thou wilt,' he cried, 'thou canst make me clean.'

Jesus looked down on the man's scaly arms and face. Then he did what no one had done to that man for long; he stretched out his hand and touched the man with his fingers.

'I will,' he said; 'be thou made clean.'

As Simon and John and the others watched, the scales went from the man's skin. He was healed of his disease. He could go and live among his people again. Despair was suddenly changed to joy. The man leapt to his feet.

'Stay,' said Jesus, who could at once see what crowds would surge round him for healing if this wonderful cure were trumpeted abroad, so that again teaching would become impossible. 'See that thou say nothing to any man. Go thy way, and shew thyself to the priest and offer for thy cleansing the things which Moses commanded' (that is, two living, clean birds, cedar-wood, and scarlet and hyssop) 'for a witness to them.'

The man, however, could not hold his tongue. He was so happy at having been healed that no sooner did he meet a man in the village to which he hurried than he began to tell his adventure.

'Jesus of Nazareth put his hands on me; at his touch I have been healed. See, my leprosy has gone. I am well: I am well.'

Just what Jesus had anticipated came to pass. If he walked into a village or town the folk swarmed out and pressed around him. They clamoured to be healed. They pleaded with him to speak to them of the Kingdom. Again and again he spent himself fighting disease. But he knew that only by teaching his group of men day by day and month by month the truth about themselves and their world, in the light of the truth about God, could his message of the Kingdom spread when (as might happen at any moment) his own voice should be silenced as John the

Baptist's already was. He went with his men along the sheep tracks and climbed into rocky, hidden desert places where he could talk to the 'little flock' as he called them sometimes, and spend time quietly in prayer with his Father. But even there, as Simon used to tell later, the crowds 'came to him from every quarter'.

CHAPTER IX

ON THE HILL TOP

ONE day of such teaching at that time they never forgot. It came about in this way. Having gone through
all Galilee, Jesus turned his face towards Capernaum,
where he had lodged with Simon. Very early one morning
he asked his men to go up into the hill that was a favourite
retreat of his. Simon, Andrew, John and some others who
were now greatly attached to him gathered on the grass
round his feet. What he said then was so simple that if a
shepherd-boy minding his flock on the hill-side loitered to
listen he could easily understand it. The men remembered
his words, so that they were able years afterwards to repeat
them to those whom they, in turn, taught and who wrote
them in the Gospels. They could remember the teaching
because it was so wonderful and so fresh.

To such boys and girls, men and women, as took hard
knocks and the sneers of superior people happily and with
a smile, Jesus declared:

'Ye are the salt of the earth.' 'But', he challenged them: 'If the
salt have lost its savour, wherewith shall it be salted? It is henceforth
good for nothing, but to be cast out and trampled under foot of men.'

To such folk as live this life of the Kingdom, he said:

'Ye are the light of the world. A city set on a hill cannot be hid,
neither do men light a lamp and put it under a bushel-measure but
on a stand; and it shineth unto all that are in the house. Even so let
your light shine before men, that they may see your good works, and
glorify your Father which is in heaven.'

John knew some of the teachers in the Temple at Jerusalem. All the young men in the group had heard the
Scribes and others teaching there at Feast times. It may
well be that one of them reminded Jesus that he had not
once in this teaching said 'Thus saith Moses', or 'These

are the words of Isaiah'; which was the way the Scribes taught.

Jesus, replying to this, went on:

'Think not that I came to destroy the law or the prophets: I came not to destroy, but to fulfil.'

He went on to give examples of the way in which, as he said, their goodness must exceed that of the Scribes and Pharisees if they were to enter into the Kingdom of heaven.

'Ye have heard that it was said to them of old time, "Thou shalt not kill"; but I say unto you that every one who is angry with his brother shall be in danger of the judgement. Ye have heard that it was said, "An eye for an eye and a tooth for a tooth": but I say unto you: "Resist not evil, but whosoever smiteth thee on thy right cheek, turn to him the other also."'

An angry Scribe might well demand—'What do you mean by saying that you do not come to destroy the Law, but to fulfil it? Here you are quoting the Law again and again and always commanding something else!'

Yet Jesus was right. For instance, the meaning of 'An eye for an eye' and 'A tooth for a tooth', was not that you must take an eye from the other man if your eye was blinded, or your tooth knocked out by his spear, but that you must *not* take more than one eye. So Jesus' command to turn the other cheek was in the real sense the completion, the fulfilment of the idea towards which that early law was a little step.

Jesus went on to give an even more difficult example:

'Ye have heard that it was said, "Thou shalt love thy neighbour and hate thine enemy": but I say unto you, "Love your enemies, and pray for them that persecute you". That ye may be sons of your Father which is in heaven: for he maketh his sun to rise on the evil and the good, and sendeth rain on the just and the unjust. For if ye love them that love you, what reward have ye? Do not even the publicans the same? And if ye salute your brethen only, what more do ye than others? Do not even the Gentiles the same? Ye therefore shall be perfect, as your Heavenly Father is perfect.'

'Take care', he said, 'not to do your good deeds in sight of men in order to attract notice.'

'When, therefore thou doest alms, sound not a trumpet before thee, as the hypocrites do in the synagogues and the streets, that they may have glory of men. Verily I say unto you, they have received their reward. But when thou doest alms, let not thy left hand know what thy right hand doeth: that thine alms may be in secret: and thy Father which seest in secret shall recompense thee. And when ye pray, ye shall not be as the hypocrites: for they love to stand and pray in the synagogues and in the corners of the streets, that they may be seen of men. Verily I say unto you, they have received their reward. But thou, when thou prayest, enter into thine inner chamber, and having shut thy door pray to thy Father which is in secret, and thy Father which seeth in secret shall recompense thee. And in praying, use not vain repetitions, as the Gentiles do: for they think they shall be heard for their much speaking. Be not therefore like unto them: for your Father knoweth what things ye have need of, before ye ask him. After this manner therefore pray ye.'

And then he taught them the Lord's Prayer.

'Our Father which art in heaven, Hallowed be thy name.
Thy kingdom come: Thy will be done in earth, as it is in heaven.
Give us this day our daily bread.
And forgive us our debts, as we forgive our debtors.
And lead us not into temptation, but deliver us from evil:
For thine is the kingdom, and the power, and the glory, for ever.
                                                    Amen.'

When he had done describing the pretences made by the hypocrites and telling his disciples how different they should be from that, he summed it all up in pictures from his old home. This made his teaching real to all who heard him, for the same things were true of their homes, where the cedar chest held its treasures and the oil lamp was burning at night on its stand.

'Lay not up for yourselves treasures upon the earth, where moth and rust doth consume, and where thieves break through and steal: but lay up for yourselves treasures in heaven, where neither moth nor rust doth consume, and where thieves do not break through nor steal: for where your treasure is, there will your heart be also. The lamp of the body is the eye: if therefore thine eye be single, thy whole body shall be full of light. But if thine eye be evil, thy whole body shall be full of darkness. If therefore the light that is in thee be darkness, how great is the darkness! No man can serve two masters: for either he will hate the one, and love the other; or else he will hold to one, and despise the other. Ye cannot serve God and mammon. Therefore I say unto you, be not anxious for your life, what ye shall eat, or what ye shall drink; nor yet for your body, what ye shall put on. Is not the life more than the food, and the body than the raiment? Behold the birds of the heaven, that they sow not, neither do they reap, nor gather into barns; and your heavenly Father feedeth them. Are not ye of much more value than they? And which of you by being anxious can add one cubit unto his stature? And why are ye anxious concerning raiment? Consider the lilies of the field, how they grow; they toil not, neither do they spin: yet I say unto you, that even Solomon in all his glory was not arrayed like one of these. But if God doth so clothe the grass of the field, which to-day is, and to-morrow is cast into the oven, shall he not much more clothe you, O ye of little faith? Be not therefore anxious, saying, What shall we eat? or, What shall we drink? or, Wherewithal shall we be clothed? For after these things do the Gentiles seek; For your heavenly Father knoweth that ye have need of all these things. But seek ye first his kingdom, and his righteousness; and all these things shall be added unto you. Be not therefore anxious for the morrow: for the morrow will be anxious for itself. Sufficient unto the day is the evil thereof.'

Then, turning from pictures of life in the home to the life of the open air, Jesus went on to a parable of the carpenter's shop. He began to teach them not to find fault with one another.

'Judge not,' he said, 'that ye be not judged. For with what judgement ye judge, ye shall be judged. And why beholdest thou the speck that is in thy brother's eye, but considerest not the timber-beam that is in thine own eye? How canst thou say to thy brother, "Brother, let me cast out the speck that is in thine eye," when thou beholdest not the beam that is in thine own eye? Thou hypocrite, cast out first the beam out of thine own eye, and then shalt thou see clearly to cast out the mote that is in thy brother's eye.'

From the workshop he turned to the farm-yard:

'Give not that which is holy to the dogs, neither cast your pearls before the swine, lest haply they trample them under their feet, and turn and rend you.'

So he turned back again to a picture of life in the home, and especially of the way a good father deals with his boys:

'Ask, and it shall be given you; seek, and ye shall find; knock, and it shall be opened unto you. For every one that asketh receiveth; and he that seeketh findeth; and to him that knocketh it shall be opened.'

'Or which of you that is a father,' he went on, 'if his son ask a loaf, will he give him a stone? Or a fish, and he for a fish give him a serpent? Or if he shall ask an egg, will he give him a scorpion?

'If ye, then, being evil, know how to give good gifts unto your children, how much more shall your heavenly Father give good things to them that ask Him?'

In one short sentence he then summed up the rule by which we should govern our behaviour:

'All things therefore whatsoever ye would that men should do unto you, even so do ye also unto them: this is the Law and the Prophets.'

Then he spoke short, swift sentences, each of which had in it a picture or a question:

'Beware of false prophets which come to you in sheepskins but within are ravening wolves. By their fruits ye shall know them. For of thorns men do not gather figs nor of a bramble bush gather they grapes, for there is no good tree that bringeth forth corrupt fruit; nor again a corrupt tree that bringeth forth good fruit. Out of the abundance of the heart the mouth speaketh, the good man out of the treasure of his heart bringeth forth that which is good; and the evil man out of the evil treasure bringeth forth that which is evil. Why call ye me "Lord, Lord?" and do not the things which I say?'

In two parables that surely came straight out of his experience as a building-carpenter at Nazareth, Jesus summed up all his teaching of that day:

'Every one that cometh unto me and heareth my words, and doeth them, I will show you to whom he is like: he is like a man, building a house, who digged and went deep, and laid a foundation upon the rock: and when a flood arose the stream brake against that house and could not shake it: because it had been well builded. But he that heareth, and doeth not, is like a man that built a house upon the earth without a foundation; against which the stream brake, and straightway it fell in, and the ruin of that house was great.'

Rising from the place where he had been seated on the hill-top, Jesus walked with his young disciples down the track into Capernaum by the Lake; but the demands of that day on his strength were not yet ended.

CHAPTER X

THE CENTURION'S SLAVE

A ROMAN officer was pacing anxiously up and down the courtyard of his house in Capernaum as Jesus ended his teaching on the hill. This centurion, who was officer over a hundred men in the Roman army of occupation, was a rich man; he could command the help of the best physicians in the city. But the doctors had failed utterly to cure his favourite servant, a slave on whom he set great store. For often Romans would be so fond of a slave that they would adopt him into the family as a son. This slave of his was dying. The centurion was wondering how to save his life. The idea of asking Jesus flashed into his mind. But how could he get word to Jesus?

The centurion was one of many Romans who, in those days, could no longer believe in the old gods like Mars, the god of war, Venus, the goddess of Love, or Jupiter, the chief of the gods. Like the Jews, he believed that there was an unseen God who had created the world and all in it. So strong was his belief that he had given of his wealth and built for the Jews the synagogue in which they worshipped in Capernaum.

He, therefore, in his desperate need hurriedly called on some of the leaders of the Jews to help him. They readily agreed, and went off to find Jesus. When he came down from the day of teaching on the hill these elders of the Jews rushed up to him.

'There is a centurion', they said to him, 'whose favourite slave is sick; indeed he is at the point of death. Will you come and heal him?' they pleaded. 'He is worthy that you should do this for him, for he loves our nation and himself built us our synagogue.'

Jesus at once started off with them towards the centurion's

house. No sooner was he seen to be going with them than people began to gather, and soon a large crowd was following him, eager to see what would happen. They were near the centurion's home when another group came hurrying toward Jesus. The centurion had sent friends of his with a message from himself to Jesus.

'Lord, trouble not thyself: for I am not worthy to come unto thee: but say the word, and my servant shall be healed. For I also am a man set under authority, having under myself soldiers: and I say to this one, Go, and he goeth; and to another, Come, and he cometh; and to my servant, Do this, and he doeth it.'

Jesus was filled with surprise as well as joy at these words. A Roman, a military officer, had this utter faith in him, faith vastly greater than he had seen among the Jews themselves. He turned round from the Roman's friends to the elders of the synagogue and the crowd of Jews behind them.

'I say unto you,' he declared, 'that I have not found so great faith, no, not in Israel.' Then the meaning of this great fact swept over him, that a man of the Roman Empire that stretched east and west, north and south, across the world, had the faith that is the gate into the Kingdom of God. 'They shall come,' Jesus cried to the crowd, 'from the east and the west, and from the north and south, and shall sit down in the Kingdom of God; when ye shall see Abraham and Isaac and Jacob, and all the prophets in the Kingdom of God and yourselves cast forth without. There shall be weeping and gnashing of teeth.'

'Behold,' he said, 'there are last which shall be first, and there are first which shall be last.'

He turned again to the friends of the centurion who were anxiously waiting his answer:

'As thou hast believed,' he replied, 'so be it done unto thee.' They hurried back to the centurion's house, and found everybody in great excitement. The slave was up and well.

Jesus returned to the house where he was staying. His disciples were with him. The elders of the synagogue who had called him to the centurion's help may have been shocked by what he had just said about men of other races than Jews going into the Kingdom of God before them. In any case, they crowded in also. The crowd gathered round the house and packed the little courtyard and the very doorway.

Those inside were surprised by a hammering in the ceiling; then the cracking of wood, and an opening was made. More surprising still, heads appeared; a mat-bed with ropes tied to the corners was let down. This was, indeed, an original way of getting past the dense crowd to Jesus. Some one must be in dead earnest. This is what had happened. A young man who was paralysed had friends who had determined to bring him before Jesus. They took their sick friend up just as he was on his mat-bed. The crowd refused to give way: they climbed the outside stair to the flat roof and, braving the anger of the owner of the house, cut a way in through it.

'My son,' said Jesus to the youth, 'be of good cheer, your sins are forgiven.'

'This man is blaspheming,' muttered one learned Scribe to his neighbour. 'Who can forgive sins but God only?'

Jesus turned on them, and said:

'Why think evil in your hearts? For whether is easier, to say "Thy sins are forgiven," or to say, "Arise and walk?" But that you may know that the Son of Man hath power on earth to forgive sins'—and with this he fixed his eyes on the young man who was ill, and said:

'Arise; and take up thy bed and go to thy house.'

Instantly the lad leapt to his feet, rolled up the bed, and shouldering it walked straight through the crowd, who, gaping with astonishment, were ready enough now to make room for him.

'Glory be to God,' they cried; and were filled with awe that such power had been given to men.

There was more room on the beach than in the house, so Jesus went and sat there. A great crowd gathered round and he taught them. As he was going back into the city he came to the cross-roads where the camel-caravans came from Persia and Damascus, from Egypt and from Caesarea on the coast with goods from Athens and Rome. The Roman government levied customs duties on the goods. Their customs officer at this place was a Jew named Levi Matthew. He belonged to the class that the Jew loathed: the tax-collectors—who drew from them the taxes levied by the Roman Government. Matthew, like most of the tax-collectors, was getting wealthy. But the words of Jesus had made a deep impression on him; he saw that there was something better in life than money-making: and when Jesus went to him and spoke the words he had already spoken to Simon and Andrew, James and John, 'Follow me,' Matthew at once left his work and went with Jesus. He called to his home many of his old friends, tax-collectors and persons who were rather careless in their ways of life, to meet Jesus and his disciples. He made a feast for them all.

Some Pharisees were furious at this:

'Why,' they asked Simon and the others, 'does your Master eat with publicans and sinners?'

Simon told Jesus about this fault-finding.

'They that are whole have no need of a physician,' said Jesus, 'but they that are sick. I came not to call righteous, but sinners.'

Some of John the Baptist's disciples were perplexed that Jesus should feast with men whose lives were wicked.

'Why,' they asked Jesus, 'do we and the Pharisees fast often, but thy disciples fast not?'

'Can the wedding-party fast,' asked Jesus, 'while the bridegroom is with them?'

Then he got to the heart of these criticisms; the real cause of offence was that he was bringing new, unheard-of teaching to the world. He tried to make it clear by recalling what used to happen when he and the other boys came home to Mary with their clothes torn by the thorn bushes or the jagged rocks of the mountain.

'No one putteth a piece of unshrunk cloth on an old garment, otherwise that which should fill it up taketh from it, the new from the old, and a worse rent is made. Neither,' he added, 'do men put new wine into old wine-skins; else the skins burst and the wine is spilled and the skins perish: but they put new wine into fresh wine-skins and both are preserved.'

CHAPTER XI

THE BOAT IN THE BAY

THE celebrated Capernaum wheat, known all over the Roman Empire for its fine flavour, was waving in the sunshine one Sabbath in May or early June. Jesus, with Simon and the others, went that morning walking through the fields which were nearly, but not quite, ready for cutting. With them were a few Pharisees. They were now eagerly watching Jesus, because he was at one and the same time immensely popular and—from their point of view—a dangerous revolutionary.

The disciples had the keen-edge hunger of young men. So they reached out their hands as they walked along and plucked ears of the wheat. They rubbed these ears in the palms of their hands, and, taking out the grain, ate it while Jesus talked with them.

'Look', grumbled a Pharisee, interrupting Jesus, 'why do your followers break the Law, doing on the Sabbath day that which is not lawful?'

How could that be a breach of the Law? For the Scroll of Deuteronomy specially said that as you walk through a cornfield you may pull ears of it to eat. But the Law forbade reaping and threshing on the Sabbath, and the Tradition of the Elders, with its hundreds of petty rules, declared that to pluck an ear of corn was a form of reaping and to roll it in the hands a form of threshing. So the disciples were blamed as law-breakers.

The Pharisees were very enthusiastic religious people, and they believed that to keep the Sabbath was the keystone which held up their faith. Murder and Sabbath-breaking deserved the same punishment—death. The Law of Moses says again and again—'whosoever works on the Sabbath shall surely be put to death'.

But Jesus asked these men who prided themselves on knowing the Sacred Scrolls by heart: 'Did you never read what David did when he had need and was an hungered, he and they that were with him? How he entered into the house of God and did eat the shewbread (that is, the twelve loaves displayed in the Temple and renewed each Sabbath), which it is not lawful to eat save for the priests, and gave also to them that were with him?'

'The Sabbath was made for man,' he declared, 'and not man for the Sabbath. The Son of Man', he added, 'is Lord of the Sabbath.'

This silenced the critics for the moment. But they had now quite made up their minds that he was a dangerous popular teacher of law-breaking.

'See,' they said to one another, 'he sets his authority above that of Moses. The other day he blasphemed; for he forgave a man's sins, which God only can do. He keeps company with tax-collectors and people who are always breaking the Law of God. Now he actually stands up for his followers when they break the Sabbath. He is more dangerous even than John the Baptist. He must be got out of the way, for he is so popular with the common people that he may do much harm leading them astray.'

Two authorities had the right to arrest a man: Herod Antipas and the Sanhedrin at Jerusalem. If they watched Jesus he was bound sooner or later to do something that would justify seizing him. That very day Jesus himself broke the Sabbath—and in the synagogue itself! Jesus went, as his custom was, to share the worship at the service. Standing there in the building was a man with a withered hand.

The Pharisees watched him.

'Will he heal this man on the Sabbath day? If so, we can accuse him.' So they whispered to one another.

'Stand forth', Jesus said to the man, looking round at

the Pharisees. He was angry that they could believe that God would rather have that man go about crippled than have him healed on the Sabbath day.

Jesus flung at them question after question that would have aroused any men with a grain of mercy.

'What man shall there be of you, that shall have one sheep and if this fall into a pit on the Sabbath day, will he not lay hold on it, and lift it out? How much then is a man of more value than a sheep! Wherefore it is lawful to do good on the sabbath day.'

They stood in chilly silence. Turning his back on them, he fixed his eyes on the man and said:

'Stretch forth thy hand.'

The man did so, and his withered hand became well and strong like the other. Imagine his joy.

Were not even the Pharisees glad? No: they hurried out of the synagogue; and joined themselves to some conspirators who were scheming to make Herod Antipas an even more powerful tyrant than he was.

They had no easy task. The whole countryside was surging with enthusiasm for Jesus. Any attempt to harm him might cause a riot. Nor could they get Pontius Pilate, with whom lay the power of life and death, to have a man killed for breaking the Law of Moses. But the enthusiasm of the crowds for Jesus might be the very means of his death. Hot-headed Galilean youths were already talking of making Jesus king. If his enemies could get up a charge against Jesus of plotting to be king and to destroy the Roman rule—then they might have him killed.

Jesus at once heard of their plot. He left Capernaum and went to a quiet place by the Lake shore. Great crowds came to him. Never before or after that time was the excitement and enthusiasm for Jesus so intense or so widespread. Simon, talking of it years after, says how he saw in those multitudes people not only from all Galilee, but from the hills of Judaea in the south, including many citizens from the capital itself, Jerusalem, and even farther south, from the wild lands of Idumaea, south of the Dead Sea, the rolling hills beyond Jordan to the east, and from the busy seaports of Tyre and Sidon on the north. It seemed impossible to describe the crowd: twice in a single sentence he repeated—as he was recalling it all to his disciple, Mark—'A great multitude, a great multitude.' The efforts of men under the spell of evil spirits and those with all sorts of diseases to get near to Jesus to touch him, became so eager and noisy that he was forced to ask Simon and Andrew to row the little boat of their fishing-trawler close to the beach ready for him to get into it if the throng grew overwhelming. He had only to touch them, for as the physician, Luke, said: 'Power came from him and healed them all.'

Jesus saw that matters had become very serious. He must have a still more closely knit band of men with him all the time and ready to go all over the land with his Good News of the Kingdom; and, above all, ready and able to continue the work even if he were killed. He went that night up to the hill-top all alone. There he prayed to his Father. He drew new strength from God after the tiring work of healing of the sick in the throng that day. Above all, he came to the decision to call the group of twelve to be with him, to have power from him to heal and to go out to preach. He sent word to those whom he wished. When he had left the earth these men were to give his teaching to the world and the story of what he was and suffered and did. He did not call learned scholars. He called rash, stumbling, warm-hearted, devoted Simon; his quieter brother, Andrew; John and James, so hot-headed and explosive that Jesus humorously called them 'The Sons of Thunder'; Matthew, the tax-collector, who turned his back on selfish cunning in order to serve the best; the other Simon, a hot-headed nationalist; the

questioning Thomas, who, however, when his doubts had
been satisfied, rose to great heights; all Galileans these;
and one southerner from Kerioth in Judaea named Judas,
a man whose love for Jesus was spoiled by jealousy and the
passion for power.

It was still early morning. They came down to Capernaum for a meal. The news that Jesus was back and
indoors brought the people flocking to the house, some
out of curiosity, others in enthusiasm for the Kingdom of
God, others for healing. So eager were the demands that
there was no time even to take food.

On the outskirts of this crowd was a strange group.
Jesus' mother and brothers in Nazareth had, like everybody else, heard the astounding stories of his doings and
his sayings. They, members of a respectable, hard-work-
ing family of working people, were told that their brother
was breaking the Sabbath—a crime to be punished by
death—teaching others to break it; eating and drinking
with rascally tax-collectors and disreputable people, and
gathering disorderly mobs round him. No wonder that
they thought he had gone mad. In any case, what he was
doing could only end in disaster and death.

So they came over the tableland and down the hill-side
to Capernaum to try to persuade him to go quietly home
with them and take up his carpenter's work again.

Meanwhile an argument was going on in the crowd.

'Is this the son of David?' asked the crowd. It only
needed a spark of certainty that he was for a flame of
patriotism to rise and for him to be proclaimed King.

'He has the power of the Prince of the Demons, Beelze-
bub,' retorted the learned Scribes, who had been sent
down from Jerusalem to discover what all the trouble was
about. 'By the prince of the devils, he casts out the devils.'

Jesus immediately turned on them and asked:

'How can Satan cast out Satan? If a kingdom be divided against itself that kingdom cannot stand. And if a house be divided against itself, that house will not be able to stand. But if I, by the Spirit of God, cast out devils, then is the Kingdom of God come upon you.'

Then, showing the great difference between the crowd and the scribes: 'He that is not with me is against me; and he that gathereth not with me scattereth.'

Word was now being passed from mouth to mouth across the crowd till it reached the centre where Jesus was surrounded by his newly selected inner group of disciples.

'Behold, thy mother and thy brothers without seek thee,' said the people to Jesus.

He knew that to the plotting of the Pharisees and the Herodians was now added this painful division with his family. So he asked sorrowfully:

'Who is my mother and my brethren?'

Then his eyes swept the circle of his faithful disciples and their friends; with Simon's wife and her mother, and Salome, the mother of John and James.

'Behold my mother and my brethren,' he answered. 'For whosoever shall do the will of God, the same is my brother, and sister, and mother.'

The spirit was on him that day to teach the multitude. But how could he reach them hemmed in by the walls of buildings? A new idea came to him. Simon's boat was ready. He went down to the beach, the crowds pressing close on his heels. There he got into the boat. The wondering multitude watched to see what would happen.

The fisher-disciples got out their oars and pulled the rowing-boat eastward near the shore round a pointed headland into a bay. The crowd tramped along the beach. Simon dropped his stone anchor in the centre of the bay, which is shaped exactly like a horseshoe with long sides and a beautiful curve in the centre, with a narrow shelving beach and banked fields behind. A man with a good voice speaking distinctly can be heard all round the bay. The crowds lined the shore, standing and sitting. The boys would be sure to get right to the front, enjoying the water lapping over their legs.

Jesus began to speak in parables. They were simple stories, which even children could take in; but with meanings which the wisest men cannot come to the end of.

'Hearken,' Jesus began, and the most restless boy was attentive.

'Behold the sower went forth to sow: and it came to pass, as he sowed, some seed fell by the wayside, and the birds came and devoured it. And other fell on rocky ground, where it had not much earth; and straightway it sprang up because it had no depth of earth: and when the sun was risen, it was scorched; and because it had no root, it withered away. And other fell among thorns, and the thorns grew up and choked them: and it yielded no fruit. And others fell into the good ground and it yielded fruit, growing up and increasing; and it brought forth thirtyfold and sixtyfold and a hundredfold. Who hath ears to hear, let him hear.'

By this he did not mean—'Let those who have brain-power grasp the meaning of this'; but—'Let those whose heart is open and whose will is to understand, take what I say into their lives.'

Jesus went on giving first a tiny story and then describing a scene, throwing new rays of light from this side and from that on the meaning of the Kingdom of God. First to show how the Kingdom grows by the secret of life from God, like wheat; but that man must first sow the seed. He said:

'So is the Kingdom of God, as if a man should cast seed upon the earth, and should sleep and rise night and day, and the seed should spring up and grow, he knoweth not how. The earth beareth fruit of herself, first the blade, then the ear, then the full corn in the ear. But when the fruit is ripe, straightway he putteth in the sickle, because the harvest is come.'

Throwing another ray of light on the same idea, he went on:

'How shall we liken the Kingdom of God? Or in what parable set

Ploughing with oxen

it forth? It is like a grain of mustard seed, which, when it is sown upon the earth though it be less than all the seeds that are upon the earth, yet when it is sown, groweth up and becometh greater than all the herbs, and putteth out great branches; so that the birds of the heaven come and lodge under the shadow thereof.'

All these pictures were part of the everyday life of all who heard him. Behind them on the hill-side were the cornfields and within sight of them the mustard-bushes, not the yellow mustard, but a tall plant that grows in the Jordan Valley as high as ten feet, although its seed is so tiny that the Jews in Palestine had and still have a pro- verbial saying: 'As small as a mustard seed.' After its brilliant yellow blossoms have faded, you may find as many as ten thousand black mustard seeds on a single bush, which are crushed as seasoning for food and for poultices; while 'the birds of the heaven', especially the linnets and goldfinches, settle in scores on its twigs to feed and rest. Any boy or girl on the beach, that afternoon, listening, would grasp at once Jesus' parable of the marvel- lous growth of life and multiplying of numbers in the Kingdom of God.

But there are other enemies to the seed than birds and rocks and shallow ground. This Jesus showed in his next story.

'The Kingdom of heaven is likened unto a man that sowed good seed in his field: but while the man slept, his enemy came and sowed tares among the wheat, and went away. But when the blades sprang up and brought forth fruit, then appeared the tares also. And the servants of the householder came and said to him, "Sir, didst not thou sow good seed in thy field? Whence, then, hath it tares?" And he said to them, "An enemy hath done this." And the servants say unto him, "Wilt thou then that we go and gather them up?" But he saith, "Nay, lest haply while ye gather up the tares, ye root up the wheat with them. Let both grow together until the harvest: and in the time of the harvest I will say to the reapers, "Gather up first the tares, and bind them in bundles to burn them, but gather the wheat into my barn."''

This parable would cause a hum of talk at once all round the bay. Every girl and woman knew the endless trouble that she had to sift the dreaded grain of the tares or darnel from the grains of wheat, which are larger. For, if cooked in the bread, it causes sickness and convulsions and even death. Every boy and man listening to Jesus knew the back-aching labour of going over every inch of a harvest-field under the broiling sun looking for this troublesome weed, which has a leaf and stalk exactly like wheat from which it cannot be picked out until the ear has actually formed.

One more tiny picture of the Kingdom of God Jesus painted for the people that afternoon, a scene taken from the life of his own home as a boy and of the home of every one there.

'The Kingdom of God is like leaven which a woman took and hid in three measures of meal till it was all leavened.'

With that he said farewell to the people. Simon turned the bow of the boat west and in a quarter of an hour it grated on the shingle. They went up into the house. As Jesus sat resting Simon and the others gathered round him and said:

'Explain unto us the parable of the tares of the field.' He replied:

'He that soweth good seed is the Son of Man; the field is the world; the good seed, these are the sons of the Kingdom; the tares are the sons of the evil one; the enemy that sowed them is the devil; the harvest is the end of the world; the reapers are the angels.'

In the same way he explained the parable of the sower:

'The sower soweth the word. And these are they by the wayside, where the word is sown; and when they heard, straightway cometh Satan, and taketh away the word which hath been sown in them. And these in like manner are they that are sown upon the rocky places, who, when they have heard the word, straightway receive it with joy; and they have no root in themselves, but endure for a while; then, when tribulation or persecution ariseth because of the word, straightway they stumble. And others are they that are sown among the thorns; these are they that have heard the word, and the cares of the world, and the deceitfulness of riches, and the lusts of other things entering in, choke the word, and it becometh unfruitful. And those are they that were sown upon good ground; such as hear the word and accept it, and bear fruit, thirtyfold, and sixtyfold, and a hundredfold.'

Then, to show his disciples the priceless value of the Kingdom of God in the heart of a man, he gave these two parables of one sentence each:

'The Kingdom of Heaven is like unto treasure hid in a field; which a man found, and hid; and in his joy he goeth and selleth all that he hath, and buyeth that field.

'Again, the Kingdom of heaven is like unto a man that is a merchant seeking goodly pearls: and having found one pearl of great price, he went and sold all that he had, and bought it.'

CHAPTER XII

THE DESPOT AND THE KINGDOM

W HEN we look back over these two days we can well
understand that Jesus was indeed tired. On the
Sabbath he had, after dealing with the Pharisees' fault-
finding with his disciples in the cornfield, healed the man
with the withered hand in face of their cold dislike, and
knowing of their plot to kill him he had spent the night,
not in sleep, but in prayer under the stars. The next morning the first thing he had done was to choose and send for
his Twelve, and then, in Capernaum, he had healed many
and suffered the criticism of his own family; after which
he had taught thousands of people in the open air, and
then explained his teaching to the Twelve. He had spent
himself. He must get a time of quiet with his Father. The
best way was to go by night across the north end of the
Lake to its eastern shore and find solitude and silence in
the hills near Gadara.

A word to Simon was enough. He had the boat ready,
with a cushion for the Master's head, so that he might
rest. Simon and Andrew, with some of the Twelve, pushed
off from the Capernaum beach in the darkness.

Without any warning, a violent gale swept down from
the north. In a few minutes the calm waters were lashed
into wild billows. These storms are common. The hot
air rises from the deep trough in which are the Lake and
the Jordan river. The cold air of Mount Hermon is sucked
down to take its place. Narrow in range, terrible in the
sudden vehemence of their rage, these storms die as swiftly
as they rise.

Simon's boat, heeling under the tempest that smote her
port side, was in great danger. She was near the shore;
but it was from the shore that the storm burst, so that she

An evening storm on the Lake of Galilee

The same scene the next morning

was driven farther out to sea. Even these hardy fishermen were frightened as the waves broke over the boat.

They could hardly believe their eyes on seeing that Jesus still slept. They gripped his arm, crying, 'Master, carest thou not that we perish?'

He awoke: 'Peace,' he said, 'Peace; be still.'

The gale ceased; the boat found herself in calm waters. He turned to them.

'Why are ye fearful: have you not yet faith?' he asked.

Marvelling they murmured to one another: 'What manner of man is this, that even the winds and the sea obey him?'

They were now near the eastern shore. On the mountain ridges was a busy Roman camp in which a legion of six thousand soldiers lived far above the heats and fevers of the Lake level, but near enough to sweep down on the rebellious Galileans if they should start a revolution.

It was now so calm that they were obliged to furl the sail and put out the oars. Soon the boat was beached at the foot of a steep hill. On a deep ledge in that mountain side was a walled city, called Gergesa; but on the beach where they landed all was lonely and quiet, except that on the steeps swineherds watched two thousand pigs grazing, being fattened for the Roman soldiery, for no Jew would eat pork. On another part of that hill was a cemetery, with its tombs hewn like shallow caves in the rock-side.

Suddenly they heard a frightful scream. A naked madman, waving his arms that were hacked with scars, his hair tangled about his face, his eyes glaring wildly, dashed at reckless speed down the steep towards Jesus. As he came nearer they could see that he had broken off the handcuffs which had been put round his wrists to prevent his doing mischief. A citizen of Gergesa, he had been driven by his madness into the loneliness of the rock-graves. Night and day in the tombs and the mountains he was crying out and cutting himself with stones.

Rushing towards Jesus, he flung himself on the ground, worshipping him.

'Thou unclean spirit,' Jesus said severely, 'come out of the man.'

'What have I to do with thee, Jesus, thou Son of the Most High God?' cried the possessed man. 'I charge you by God, torment me not.'

'What is thy name?' Jesus demanded.

'Legion,' he replied, 'for we are many.'

To a Gergesene citizen under the shadow of the Roman camp, legion was the natural word to describe a great number, and the poor madman felt as though many demons were struggling within him.

And then that great herd of pigs rushed headlong into the sea, while the man sat quietly by Jesus on a boulder. The panic-stricken swineherds raced to the city. They told their masters that Jesus had sent a legion of demons out of the madman into their beasts, which had dashed into the sea and were drowned. The populace hastened out and saw the man sane and the pigs drowned. They were terror-stricken by the strange event, and besought Jesus to leave the neighbourhood. The man who was healed, however, asked Jesus to let him join his disciples and be with him.

'Return to thy house,' replied Jesus, 'and declare how great things God hath done for thee, and how he had mercy on thee.'

So the man went his way, and told throughout the city the story of what wonderful things Jesus had done for him.

Through this strange adventure, Jesus' desire to escape into a peaceful place had again been foiled. For the wish of the foolish Gergesenes on the eastern shore of the Lake to get rid of Jesus was surpassed by the eagerness of the dense waiting crowds on the north-western beach that he should hasten back to them. Simon steered his little boat homeward. No sooner had the keel grated on the shingle than the people thronged round Jesus. He seated himself close to the water's edge.

A man came elbowing his way through the mob. Jesus recognized him. It was a ruler of the Capernaum synagogue; he had more than once called on Jesus to read and speak.

'My little daughter,' said Jairus, 'is at the point of death: I pray thee that thou come and lay thy hands on her and she shall live.'

To give life to a girl, to bring joy to a father, crazed with grief: Jesus could not refuse to do this. He rose and side by side with Jairus moved towards his house. The crowd was so dense that one of Jesus' men, describing the experience, said that they were 'ground as between millstones'.

Jesus unexpectedly stopped. Looking round he asked: 'Who touched my clothes?'

Simon, bewildered at this apparently senseless demand, exclaimed:

'Master; the multitudes press thee and crush thee; and sayest thou "Who touched me?"'

'But some one did touch me,' said Jesus; 'for I perceive that power has gone forth from me.'

His eyes continued to search the faces in the crowd. Suddenly a woman darted forward. She fell on her knees in front of him.

'I have been ill for twelve years,' she said. 'I have spent all my money on many physicians. None could heal me. So I came behind thee and touched the hem of thy garment. I was healed immediately.'

'Daughter,' said Jesus with gentle courtesy, 'thy faith hath made thee whole. Go in peace.'

As they started again towards Jairus' house, a grief-stricken friend came hurrying through the crowd.

'Thy daughter is dead,' he said to Jairus. 'Trouble not the Master.'

This was terrible news to Jairus. But Jesus turned to him and said:

'Fear not, only believe, and she shall be made whole.'

So they came at last to the house. Already the mourners were playing the flutes of grief. The women were wailing. The men, smiting on their breasts, broke into loud laments.

'Give place,' cried Jesus. 'Why make ye a tumult and weep? The child is not dead, but sleepeth.'

At this they laughed scornfully. Jesus told Jairus to send them away; then, taking with him the three men whom he kept close by him (as we shall see) on other high occasions—Simon, James, and John—he went with Jairus and his wife to the bed where the girl lay.

'*Talitha cumi*' (little lamb), he said, 'arise.'

She opened her eyes, smiled at her father and mother, and stood on her feet. Joyfully they threw their arms around her. Jesus said:

'Give her something to eat.'

Jesus now felt a desire to go back to see the people in his home town. So he led his men for fifteen miles across the little Plain of Gennesaret up the Way of the Sea, through the fields and the villages on the hills to Nazareth.

As his custom was, Jesus went on the Sabbath to the synagogue. There, in the building where he had worshipped as a boy and a young working-man, the leaders of the worship asked their fellow citizen to read the lesson from the Scroll of the Prophet and to speak to them.

The Keeper of the Books took the Scroll of the Prophet Isaiah and placed it in his hands. Unrolling it, Jesus found the place where it is written:

'The Spirit of the Lord God is upon me,
Because He anointed me to preach good tidings to the poor.
He hath sent me to proclaim release to the captives.
And recovery of sight to the blind,
To set at liberty them that are bruised,
To proclaim the acceptable year of the Lord.'

He closed the book. He had stopped at that point in the middle of a sentence, and did not go on to read the words that were not true of himself—'And the day of vengeance of our God'.

He sat down. The eyes of every one in the synagogue were riveted on him.

'To-day,' he declared, 'hath this scripture been fulfilled in your ears.'

They were overwhelmed. Simon, in telling Mark about it, used the strongest word in the language for intense astonishment. Some wondered at the grace of the words that he then spoke. But most were offended.

'Whence hath this man these things?' they asked. 'What is the wisdom given to this man? What mean such mighty works wrought by his hands? Is not this the carpenter? Is not this Joseph's son, the son of Mary, and brother of James and Joses, Judas and Simon? Are not his sisters here with us?'

How could the man who had made their door-posts and ploughs and ox-yokes be the Servant of God to bring His Good News to the poor, free those in prison, break the fetters of those under harsh tyranny? How could that be true of one whom they had seen for nearly thirty years growing up and then working to keep his mother and the younger ones? That was not their idea of the way God's Anointed would come. It must be that either he was out of his mind, or he was an upstart impostor.

They were more sure of this because Jesus could not do any mighty work such as he had only a few days before performed at Capernaum.

'Doubtless you will say to me,' said Jesus, 'Physician, heal thyself: whatsoever we have heard done at Capernaum, do also here in thine own country.'

'Truly a prophet is not without honour,' he continued sadly, 'save in his own country, and among his own family and in his own home.'

He went on in words that would, indeed, be bitter to a company of Jews, to show that Elijah, when there was famine in the land, was sent out to the widow in Phoenicia, a pagan Sidonese, right outside the Jewish boundary; that Elisha was sent to heal, not any of the multitude of Jewish lepers, but a distinguished officer in the army of their enemies, the Syrians.

As he went on the fury of the Nazarenes in the synagogue rose to boiling-point. Unable to contain themselves, they rushed at him and hauled him along up the hill towards a precipice over which they were going to hurl him into the ravine below. Their nerve failed. Why, we do not know. There was the Roman camp not far away to call them to account for murder. There was that in him, in what he said and what he was, that might well make them wonder whether, after all, God's power might be with him. And if he were right, how terrible was their blind crime! So he went out with his men from the place of his boyhood, never to return.

How different was the welcome, as he strode once more into Capernaum! Crowds flocked to him. Some longed for the coming of the Kingdom of God, that they might be freed from pain and sorrow. The younger men, hating the hard rule of Herod Antipas in Galilee and even the milder sway of his brother, Philip, just north-east of the Lake; loathing above all the cold, stern rule of Rome through Pontius Pilate; hoped that Jesus might raise the banner of revolt and in the power of God—which, alone, could conquer Rome—drive the Legions into the sea as the swine had gone at Gadara. Others desired to be set free from evil thoughts and desires.

The leaders of Jewish religion in the synagogue and in the Temple gave them no help in these things. They only vexed the people with rules of no real importance and with the heavy costs of sacrifice. Jesus went unresting up and down the highways and by-ways of Galilee. Everywhere the same clamorous need. To him the people were as sheep wandering on the hills, distressed and scattered, amid jackals and wolves, with no shepherd.

He looked at the crowds; he looked at the Twelve.

'The harvest,' he said, pointing to the crowds, 'is plenteous. But,' and his eyes searched his little group, 'the labourers are few. Pray the Lord of the harvest,' he bade them, 'that he send forth labourers into His harvest.'

How could that prayer be answered? The Twelve were to be God's first answer to it. They had been pupils—disciples: let them now be teachers, messengers, apostles. He gave them power to cast out evil spirits and to heal disease.

'Go not into any way of the Gentiles,' he said, 'and enter not into any city of the Samaritans: but go rather to the lost sheep of the house of Israel.'

Why should they go only to Jews? It was an instruction for that special journey. First, they were not trained yet for telling the Good News to people of other nations and religions. Secondly, speed was necessary. Thirdly, and most vital of all, the Jews with their knowledge of the One Holy, Almighty God (which no other nation then had) were spread all over the Roman Empire and beyond it. So they were prepared in a way that was true of no other people to receive the Good News of the Kingdom of God.

'As ye go,' continued Jesus, 'preach; saying, "The Kingdom of Heaven is at hand." Heal the sick, cleanse the lepers, cast out devils.

'Ye have received without payment, give without reward.

'Take nothing for your journey, save only a staff. No bread, no wallet, no money in your purse; but go shod with sandals: and,' said he, 'put not on two coats.'

The two things they were told to take—the staff and the sandals—were both necessary for speed.

'Into whatever city or village ye enter, search out in it who is worthy. Abide there till ye go forth. As ye enter into the house salute it with "Shalom"—"Peace." If the house be worthy your peace will come upon it; if not, it will return to you. And whosoever shall not receive you nor listen to your words, as ye go forth from that house or that city, shake off the dust of your feet.

'Behold,' he warned them, 'I send you forth as sheep in the midst of wolves: be ye therefore wise as serpents and harmless as doves. But beware of men: for they will deliver you up to the councils, and they will scourge you in their synagogues; and ye shall be brought before governors and kings for my sake.' With other warnings he prepared them to expect that the adventure would be full of peril and hardship; but that God would watch over them.

'Are not five sparrows sold for two farthings? And not one of them is forgotten in the sight of God? But the very hairs of your head are numbered. Fear not: Ye are of more value than many sparrows.'

Very difficult were some of his sayings to them:

'Think not that I came to send peace on earth: I came not to send peace, but a sword. For I came to set a man at variance against his father, and the daughter against her mother. A man's foes shall be those of his own household. He that loveth father or mother more than me is not worthy of me, and he that loveth son or daughter more than me is not worthy of me.'

By this he did not, of course, mean that he wished for fathers and sons to quarrel about him. He did mean, as he had found with his own family, that any one who followed him and lived as he would have them live would certainly find himself attacked by those who lived as though getting things for oneself were the aim in life. In that sense the Kingdom of God must bring, 'not peace, but a sword'.

He cheered them greatly by his wonderful word:

'He that receiveth you, receiveth me, and he that receiveth me receiveth him that sent me. And whosoever shall give to drink unto one of these little ones a cup of cold water only in the name of a disciple, verily I say unto you he shall in no wise lose his reward.'

He sent them away in all directions. Simon and Andrew, the brothers, he told to go one way; the other brothers, James and John, in another direction. Philip of Bethsaida had as companion Nathanael, while Matthew went with Thomas. The other James, son of Alphaeus, went with a disciple named Lebbaeus Thaddeus. And Judas Iscariot with the other Simon, called for his fiery patriotism, the Zealot.

Jesus himself started out alone to concentrate on the cities of the land, where he preached and healed.

Meanwhile, John the Baptist lived on in the prison of Machaerus Castle, on the high, harsh precipice beyond the Dead Sea. Far from the happenings around Capernaum he began to be tormented by doubts whether Jesus really was God's Messiah. The gossip that he heard about Jesus from his own disciples, whom Herod Antipas allowed to visit him, distressed John. He had lived on very little, simple food—honey taken from the wild bees' nest, and locusts; and water from a wayside spring. Jesus, he heard, was banqueting with rich tax-gatherers and wine-bibbing sinners. John had proclaimed the 'Wrath to come' on those who did not repent. Jesus spoke of the Kingdom of God as a plant growing silently or as yeast changing the flour in secret, and was calling on men to love even those who attacked them. Was this really the Messiah of whom

John was to be the Forerunner, or must they still await his coming?

At last John sent two of his disciples to find Jesus and put this question to him: 'Art thou he that should come, or do we look for another?'

These men came northward up the Jordan Valley caravan route to the Lake of Galilee and then along its western shore till, by the sea close to the town of Magdala, not far from Capernaum, they saw an immense crowd of people. Pressing through they at last found Jesus in the centre of the crowd. He was healing a sick man. When he turned to them they told him their errand.

'Art thou he that should come, or look we for another?'

Jesus, instead of replying at once, went on with his work. A blind man came, and Jesus, touching his eyes, restored his sight. Another, tormented with demon-possession, was put into his right mind. One after another was healed and went away rejoicing. He spoke to the people of the coming of the Kingdom of God, the Rule of the Father of love and purity, peace and justice. Then Jesus turned and spoke to the wondering disciples of John. Nor did he use an argument of his own. He quoted in part the words from the prophet Isaiah that showed what the work of the Messiah would be.

'Go your way,' he said, 'and tell John, what things ye have seen and heard; "the blind receive their sight", the lame walk, the lepers are cleansed, the deaf hear, the dead are raised up, the "poor have good tidings preached to them". And', he added, turning to his own disciples about him, 'blessed is he, whosoever shall find none occasion of stumbling in me.'

So the men left him and returned to John. And then Jesus went on to speak to the crowd of John himself:

'What went ye into the wilderness to see' he asked. 'A reed shaken in the wind? But what went ye out to see? A man clothed in soft raiment? Behold they which are gorgeously apparelled, and live delicately, are in King's courts. But what went ye out to see?'

It seems as though some voice from among the people must have answered his question, 'A prophet'.

'A prophet?' Jesus replied; 'Yea, I say unto you, and much more than a prophet. This is he of whom it is written, "Behold, I send my messenger before thy face, who shall prepare thy way before thee", I say unto you, among them that are born of women there is none greater than John: yet he that is but little in the Kingdom of God is greater than he.'

The people in the crowd murmured their agreement with his praise of John; indeed, many of them had followed him and been baptized by him in Jordan. But the Pharisees growled their disapproval, and Jesus turned upon them. 'Whereunto shall I liken this generation; and to what are they like?' he asked, pointing to this group of critics from Jerusalem.

'They are like unto children that sit in the market-place and call to one another; which say: "We piped unto you, and ye did not dance; we wailed, and ye did not weep." For John the Baptist is come neither eating nor drinking; and ye say: "He hath a devil." The Son of Man came eating and drinking, and ye say, "Behold a gluttonous man and a wine bibber, A friend of publicans and sinners!" Nevertheless wisdom is vindicated by all her children.'

As Jesus turned from the cold, sneering Pharisees to the crowd of unlettered people, and especially to his own little group of disciples, who grasped his message so much more swiftly than these learned men, he raised his face to heaven and said:

'I thank Thee, O Father, Lord of Heaven and earth, that thou didst hide these things from the wise and understanding, and didst reveal them unto babes: yea, Father, for so it was well-pleasing in thy sight.'

Then he turned again to these simple people toiling with their hands for a living, and he cried out to them:

'Come unto me, all ye that labour and are heavy-laden, and I will give you rest. Take my yoke upon you; and learn of me; for I am

meek and lowly in heart: and "ye shall find rest for your souls" . . .
for my yoke is easy, and my burden is light.'

While Jesus was thus teaching near Magdala, one of
the Pharisees, named Simon, more from curiosity than
kindliness, asked him if he would eat with him.

Jesus went to the man's house. So little did Simon really
respect this travelling teacher from the working class that
he did not even carry out the ordinary kindly courtesies
that every man payed his guest in the East. For a servant
would remove the sandals, wash the dust of the road from
the feet before the guest reclined on his couch at the low
table, and would refresh the guest by dropping perfume
on his head, while the host gave him the kiss of friendliness.
Simon did none of these things.

Jesus, undoing his own sandals, took his place at the
table and the meal began. In that hot valley the sheltered
dining-arbour was not enclosed, but open to the courtyard
of the house. In the twilight a woman had already come
softly through the quadrangle and stood behind Jesus'
couch, facing Simon. She had lived a sinful life; but she
had seen in Jesus and had heard in his words such purity
and mercy that her life was cleansed. Her sorrow for her
bad past; her love for Jesus sent tears flowing down her
cheeks. They dropped upon his dusty feet and she kissed
them and wiped them with her hair. Then she opened
a little jar of ointment. The ointment was costly, the jar
was carved of alabaster. She poured this gift upon his feet.

Simon looked on in chilly silence. He was saying within
himself. 'This man, if he were the prophet, would have
perceived who and what manner of woman this is which
toucheth him, that she is a sinner.'

Jesus, reading him like an open scroll, looked up from
his food and said:

'Simon, I have somewhat to say to thee.'

'Say on, Master,' answered Simon curtly.

'A certain money-lender,' Jesus pursued quietly, 'had two debtors: the one owed five hundred pence, the other fifty. When they had not wherewith to pay, he forgave them both. Which of them, therefore, will love him the most?'

'I suppose,' replied Simon, with a sneer, perhaps, at this simple question, 'he to whom he forgave most.'

'Thou hast rightly judged,' Jesus answered, and then rebuked his discourteous host with a directness of speech that must have made even the smug Pharisee uncomfortable.

Turning his eyes from Simon to the woman, Jesus said to him: 'Seest thou this woman? I entered into thine house, thou gavest me no water for my feet: but she hath wetted my feet with her tears, and wiped them with her hair. Thou gavest me no kiss: but she, since the time I came in, hath not ceased to kiss my feet. My head with oil thou didst not anoint: but she hath anointed my feet with ointment.

'Wherefore, I say unto thee, her sins, which are many, are forgiven; for she loved much: but' (and his glance now fell full on Simon) 'to whom little is forgiven, the same loveth little.'

Turning again to the woman, he said: 'Thy sins are forgiven.'

The other guests at the feast murmured to one another, scandalized, 'Who is this that even forgiveth sins?'

To the woman, still waiting in the shadow, he said a gracious farewell: 'Thy faith hath saved thee; go in peace.'

So the supper ended.

Jesus and the Twelve went on their way. Some women whom Jesus had healed walked as disciples with Him and the Twelve. One of them was Joanna, the wife of Herod Antipas' chief officer of state, Chuza; another was called Susanna, and a third (was it the woman of the supper?) was Mary of Magdala, out of whom, they said, he had cast seven devils.

These women were helping Jesus and the Twelve, they believed in him and loved him, because he had changed their lives. Another woman, however, at the other end of the Jordan Valley, in spite was plotting to bring John the Baptist to his death. She was inwardly raging because John, in his blunt, daring way had told Herod to his face the truth, that his marriage to Herodias, whom he had taken from his half-brother to whom she was already married, was a shameful sin. Herod himself knew in his soul that John was right. He would call John to him to hear him talk of the Kingdom of God, and always John made his conscience tremble. Herod had the good and the bad ways of an Oriental despot. One day he gave a great feast to his nobles, his generals, his judges, and other important people. Wine was plentiful. Herod drank deeply. Herodias' daughter came and danced. The guests were so charmed with her loveliness and her graceful dancing that Herod swore that he would give her anything she asked, up to half his kingdom.

'What shall I ask?' she asked her mother.

Herodias' eyes gleamed with hate. 'The head of John the Baptist,' said the revengeful woman.

The girl made her horrible demand. The drunken king was like a rabbit in the snare: he could not escape the consequences of his rash promise. He dared not break his oath or he would be the laughing-stock of his guests and the whole country. So he gave the order to his executioner. John's head was struck off. His disciples carried him away for burial. Herod's heart was heavy, but he was at any rate rid of a troublesome agitator. But he was to have no peace. Men came down the Jordan Valley from the north end of the Lake.

'Multitudes like the sand of the sea shore,' they declared to Herod, 'are gathering around a new prophet who, while he heals the sick and gives sight to the blind, proclaims to the people the coming of the Kingdom of God.'

Superstitious Herod, full of dread, cried: 'John the Baptist, whom I beheaded, has risen from the dead.'

Others came to Herod saying: 'No, it is Elijah, who has come again as the Scriptures foretold.'

Herod, we are told, was bewildered; he 'was quite at a loss'. He was, in fact, desperately disturbed. The crowds, so dense that they trampled on one another, were listening to 'the Good Tidings of the Kingdom'. Well, but Herod himself was king—under the Emperor Tiberius, who was far away in Rome. Still worse, Jesus had sent Twelve firebrands all over Herod's territory, and the message that he told them to declare was—'The Kingdom of God is at hand'.

Herod made up his mind that he must seize his chance to put Jesus in prison.

Jesus was not afraid to die.

He saw that his enemies were beginning to close round him in order to have him put to death. But he was clear that, when he came to die, it must be at the centre of national life, and at the only time in the year when the whole nation was gathered there. It must, in a word, be in Jerusalem and at the Passover. The time was not yet. Jesus, therefore, determined to leave the territory where Herod's orders ran, and to cross into the land ruled by his milder, juster brother, Philip.

CHAPTER XIII

COMRADES OF THE OPEN ROAD

THE Twelve gathered round Jesus eager to tell him their adventures—what they had done and what they had taught, how the people had received them, the wonders that had come to pass. But there was such a hubbub and bustle of people coming and going that they could neither tell Jesus what they wanted, nor could they find time even to eat.

'Come apart unto a desert place,' said Jesus, 'and rest awhile.'

Climbing aboard Simon's fishing-smack they trimmed her sails and set the helm over to run her along the north shore of the Lake eastward. Soon they passed the inflow of the Jordan river. From that point eastward Herod had no power: his brother Philip governed. They were both sons of Herod the Great. As there were comparatively few Jews in Philip's part of the country he had no fear of revolutionary upheavals.

Beautiful green grass, a rare sight in that land, greeted the eyes of Jesus and the Twelve as they gazed from the ship over a little plain called Buthaiha, fringed on the north and east by hills. Along its western side ran the Jordan, by which was a little town which Philip had recently rebuilt, another fisher-home, called Bethsaida Julias in honour of the Emperor Tiberius' daughter. Landing on the coast of this little plain each man of the Twelve took his basket full of provisions, such as the Jews carried according to Moses' instructions when travelling in places where there are few Jews, and where it was, therefore, difficult to get food which had been chosen, killed, and cleansed according to the Law. These baskets Jesus told them not to carry, you remember, when they were going out two by two to Jews only, among whom they could get this kind of food. But when going into a desert place and among people who were not Jews, it was necessary that they should carry their baskets.

They walked across the plain, and on its northern edge where the rocks began they rested and took food. Here, at last, was peace and quietness. They began to talk with their Master over their experiences. Judge how startled and annoyed the apostles were when they saw masses of men and women, boys and girls, hurrying towards them. The people had seen which way Simon's boat sailed. They feared that Jesus was leaving their land, and they determined to make him their king at once. So they came wading across the ford of the upper Jordan and hastening over the plain toward Jesus and the Twelve.

But it was not anger at being interrupted that Jesus felt as he saw over five thousand folk hurrying towards him. 'The people,' Simon said later, when dictating the story to Mark, 'ran there together on foot from all the cities and outwent us. . . . And Jesus had compassion on them, because they were "as sheep not having a shepherd".'

Jesus drew the crowd towards him; and seated on some slope where he could be seen and heard, he taught them many things. The day wore on. The disciples grew restless.

'This place is desert,' they said to him. 'The day is now far spent. Send them away, that they may go into the country and the villages round about and buy themselves somewhat to eat.' The supplies in their baskets were exhausted.

'Give ye them to eat,' replied Jesus.

'Philip,' he said, turning to the native of Bethsaida, who knew all the resources of the villages, 'whence are we to buy bread that these may eat?'

'Shall we go and buy two thousand pennyworth of food?'

they asked. 'Even that,' Philip reckoned, 'would not be enough for each to have a little.'

'How many loaves have you now?' asked Jesus. 'Go and see.'

Andrew, Simon's brother, had already been making inquiries. He had found a boy with a little food in his satchel.

'There is a lad here who has five barley loaves and two small fishes,' he said, 'but what,' he asked helplessly, 'is that among so many?'

'Make the people sit down in companies upon the green grass,' Jesus commanded. The people were arranged in hundreds and fifties by the apostles. Jesus took the food and with his face lifted to heaven, blessed the loaves and fishes and broke them in his hands. He then handed the pieces to the disciples. They went among the multitude, men and women, boys and girls, and fed them. When all were satisfied, Jesus sent the Twelve to collect what was left. Each came back with his basket full.

The pent-up feeling of the people could be held back no longer. As Moses had fed the Israelites in the desert, so Jesus now would feed them and would lead them into the Promised Land of a Jewish Kingdom of God, free from the rule of Rome.

'This is of a truth the prophet that was to come into the world,' they cried.

They hastened towards him, eager, as Jesus knew, to take him by force and make him King. It was now dusk. He persuaded the crowd to leave him while he went into the mountain to pray. The disciples he sent down to the beach to start back home to Capernaum.

In the silence on the hill-top he came to a new decision. He must get away from the multitude and still further teach his men how to carry the Good Tidings of the Kingdom of God to the world, when he should be gone. Herod had just killed John the Baptist and was inquiring where Jesus was. The Pharisees and Scribes were weaving their schemes under the eyes of Annas and Caiaphas in the Temple. From this point on he rarely was in Capernaum or among the crowds or in Herod's lands.

Leaving the mountain, Jesus strode through the darkness down to the plain. A storm was blowing up. By the time he reached the shore the wind was beating the waves into foaming wrath. He could just see the boat in which were the men on whom he relied to carry on his work. Toiling at the oars they strained every sinew; but all in vain. Jesus, walking westward along the beach, turned and made straight out towards them. They saw his form in the darkness and taking it for that of a spirit, cried out in terror.

'Be of good cheer,' the voice they knew so well rang out across the water; 'it is I; be not afraid.'

He reached the boat and stepped over the gunwale. The wind ceased. They were overcome with awe. They sailed by Capernaum to the beach by the Plain of Gennesaret. There they moored the boat. Jesus landed and the news of his presence was at once widely spread. Sick folk were carried out on their mat-beds and laid in the village market-places as he passed through. He went into Capernaum at one time in this short period of healing and teaching and there he was drawn into a dangerous argument by some Scribes whom Caiaphas and the Sanhedrin at Jerusalem had sent down.

'Why walk not thy disciples by the Torah, the Tradition of the Elders, for they wash not their hands when they eat bread?'

They thought that this question was bound to lead Jesus into a trap. If he defended the disciples, he was a breaker of the Law of Moses, and was open to punishment by the Sanhedrin; if he said that his disciples were wrong, then they had shown him and them to be law-breakers. But Jesus turned to them and said:

'Well did Isaiah say of you hypocrites: "This people honoureth me with their lips. But their heart is far from me. . . ." Ye leave the commandment of God, and hold fast the Tradition of Men. For Moses said "Honour thy father and thy mother;" but ye say: "Whoever shall say to his father or his mother, 'That wherewith thou mightest have been profited by me is "Corban", that is, "given to God",' he need not honour his father".'

The Scribes and Pharisees left him, baffled and furious in their hearts.

The Temple rulers, the very head of the Jewish nation, were massed against Jesus and plotting his death. So he could not go south into Judaea.

'Herod is planning to kill you,' some Pharisees told Jesus. 'Get away from here.'

They might well say so, for Herod's golden palace at Tiberias was not an hour's ride from Capernaum.

Thus the people left him because he refused to head a Jewish revolution, and Herod wanted to kill him as a dangerous revolutionary.

'Go and tell that fox,' answered Jesus, putting all Herod's slinking, cowardly, treacherous ways into that one word, 'To-day and to-morrow I cast out evil spirits and I heal; the next day my work is done. Yet,' he added, 'I must travel on to-day and to-morrow and the next day. It would not be fitting,' he concluded ironically, 'that a prophet should die outside Jerusalem.'

Avoiding Judaea on the south and leaving Galilee, Jesus with his men struck the track to the north. It was a bracing climb from the heats of the Lake side, six hundred feet below sea-level, to the ridges west of Mount Hermon, from which they could see the Mediterranean two thousand feet below them. Moving down the winding valleys towards the coast they came to the ancient city of Tyre that sent its daring seamen to lands far away.

They found a house on the outskirts of Tyre where they could stay quietly. There Jesus could go on with the work of preparing his men for their great mission.

But even in that quiet, secluded spot Jesus was not to remain undisturbed. A woman who was in terrible trouble because her little daughter was possessed by an evil spirit discovered that the great prophet was there, he of whom Phoenician merchants had brought back marvellous news from the market at Capernaum. Some of the people from this coast he had actually healed by the Lake of Galilee and they had heard him preaching the Good Tidings there.

So anxious were the Twelve to keep the woman away that they tried repeatedly, when she followed them, to get her to leave. But she was so desperate about her daughter that she would not go. She was not of Hebrew blood; indeed she was a Greek-speaking native of this Phoenician part of Syria.

At last, when Jesus was in the courtyard of the house taking food with his friends, she made her way into the place. Near the table, as was usual, there were some dogs on the look-out for scraps to eat.

'Have mercy on me, O Lord, thou son of David,' she cried, 'my daughter is grievously vexed by a devil.'

'Send her away,' said his disciples, 'for she crieth after us.'

'Lord, help me,' she cried again.

'I am sent to the lost sheep of the house of Israel,' said Jesus. 'It is not right to take the children's bread and throw it to the dogs.'

She was looking into his eyes: she could see behind his words the tenderness in his heart; and so she pointed to the dogs.

'Yea, Lord,' she replied, 'but even the dogs eat of the crumbs that fall from their master's table.'

Her ready wit, her belief in his will and his power to help, pleased Jesus

'O woman,' he cried, 'great is your faith: be it done unto thee even as thou wilt.'

The Twelve and their Master once more took the northward road. A full day's walk northward, not far from the coast, carried them across the Leontes river to the wealthy shipping port of Sidon. They did not stay there long, but turned eastward inland. They climbed the slopes of the hills and crossed deep ravines in which the tributaries of the upper Jordan come down from Mount Hermon. They walked along tracks where few men came. On the way, Simon and Andrew, James and John, Thomas and Matthew, and the others, told Jesus of their successes, their failures, the unexpected difficulties that they had met on their journeys two by two through the villages and the cities of Galilee. Their stories enabled Jesus to tell them how to overcome the obstacles, avoid the failures, multiply the successes, and to lead them into deeper and deeper understanding of God and His will for them and for the world of men.

At last they climbed to a rolling highland country that spread to the north and the south mostly on the east side of the Jordan Valley called 'The Land of Ten Cities.' This name came from the fact that in that very fruitful region, where orchards bloomed and large flocks of sheep and herds of camels and goats grazed, ten rich Greek cities had grown up from the time when Alexander the Great passed that way from Greece with his armies.

Jesus had been on the edge of this land of Decapolis (or Ten Cities) before; for Gadara, by the Lake of Galilee, where the man who called himself 'Legion' lived, was one of them. In it the Greek gods were worshipped. Gladiators fought and chariot races were run in the marble amphitheatre; and there was a noble aqueduct thirty miles long that carried running water to its streets. Here his fame had already spread, and though he wished to avoid crowds and have leisure for teaching the Twelve, these people came to see him and to hear his wonderful words.

Jesus and the Twelve presently began to work their way round towards Galilee again. No sooner did they come near its shores than they were again attacked by the Pharisees for not carrying out all the forms of the Law and the Tradition of the Elders. It was clear that there could be no rest for him at Capernaum; for no sooner had his boat reached the Bethsaida fishing bay than a blind man was brought to him to heal. Jesus, again anxious to avoid gathering a crowd, led the blind man from the village to the edge of the orchards. Then he made spittle. He put it on the eyes of the man and laid his fingers on him.

'Canst thou see anything?' he asked.

The man, in great excitement, exclaimed, 'I can see men—but dimly like trees walking.'

Again Jesus laid his hands on him. Now he saw quite distinctly.

'Go to your home now,' said Jesus, 'do not even go into this village.'

Once more, and for the last time, he led his men northward into the quiet places among the hills. This time, however, they did not take the merchant-trails towards Tyre, but the route that led towards Damascus. They followed the upper Jordan from the Lake to the Bridge of the Daughters of Jacob. When once they had gained the eastern side of that bridge they were remote from all danger of imprisonment, for they were again under Philip's rule. Slowly climbing, they passed the marshy waters of Lake Huleh, ten miles from the Lake of Galilee, yet seven hundred feet above its level.

The way was now steeper. They climbed another two thousand feet and more. Jesus was thinking of what he must do and of how his work would fare in the future. At one place high among the hills he left his men and turned aside a little way to pray to his Father, for there was great need of strength and of light to see what he must do.

The rulers and the priests were against him. Of the crowds, many who had thought to follow him had turned back because he would not lead them in revolt against their Roman rulers. They still did not understand the real meaning of his teaching.

Going back to his men Jesus put to them two questions; the answers to which were for him, as we shall see, very important.

'Who do men say that I am?' he asked.

'John the Baptist,' they replied, 'but some say Elijah, and others say that you are Jeremiah or one of the prophets, who has risen again.'

'And who do you say that I am?'

Simon, in his impulsive, downright way, cried, 'The Christ, the Son of the Living God.'

Jesus' joy was great.

'Blessed art thou, Simon, son of John,' he cried. 'For flesh and blood hath not revealed it unto thee, but my Father which is in heaven. And I also say unto thee that thou art Petros, and upon this Petros, this rock, will I build my church; and the gates of Hades shall not prevail against it. I will give unto thee the keys of the Kingdom of Heaven: and whatsoever thou shalt bind on earth shall be bound in heaven, and whatsoever thou shalt loose on earth shall be loosed in heaven.'

'Do not tell any one now that I am the Christ,' Jesus said to them: for the time had not yet come.

Jesus in these days of quiet began to get his men ready for what must lie ahead. He could see that the Pharisees' hate in Galilee was only the spear-head of the cold enmity of Annas and Caiaphas at Jerusalem, who had sent group after group down to spy on him and to try to catch him out so that they could bring against him a charge that would involve his death. Sooner or later they would succeed. Only one person could pronounce the death-sentence: the Roman Governor; and that meant—as Jesus was not a Roman citizen—the cruel death on the cross. How could he break the prospect of all this to his Twelve, who worshipped him?

'I must go to Jerusalem,' Jesus explained to them, 'and suffer many things of the elders and chief priests and Scribes, and be killed, and the third day be raised up.'

Jesus to be killed! Peter's worship and love for his Master made this incredible news impossible to endure. Impulsively he gripped hold of his Lord and led him apart.

'Be it far from thee, Lord,' he cried: 'this shall never be unto thee.'

Jesus, listening to this voice of his disciple calling him to an easier path, recognized in it just the same temptation that had come to him over a year ago in the wilderness. Therefore he cried out:

'Get thee behind me, Satan! Thou art a stumbling-block unto me. Thou mindest not the things of God, but the things of men.'

He went on to make his meaning clearer.

'If any man would come after me,' he said, 'let him deny himself and take up his cross and follow me. For whosoever would save his life shall lose it, and whosoever shall lose his life for my sake shall find it. For what shall it profit a man to gain the whole world and forfeit his life, or what shall a man give in exchange for his life?'

Simon and Andrew, listening to these words, could not have foreseen that within a few years they, among the first of Jesus' disciples, should suffer death for his sake.

Jesus was at this time near the foot of Mount Hermon. It was so early in the year that the white turban of snow that makes the people call this majestic mountain 'the Sheikh' was not yet melted.

Here they spent some six days walking on the mountain

sides; then Jesus, taking with him his three closest friends, Peter, James, and John, began to climb still higher. So they came to the strong shoulder of Hermon where, when the mists swept away, the splendour of the sun lighted a marvellous landscape. Jesus went to that high place to pray. Going a space apart from his followers, he knelt in communion with his Father.

There, in the night, while his tired young disciples slept on the sparse turf, he faced the agony ahead of him. He prayed for the coming of the Kingdom of God in men's lives, for which he was to pay so great a price.

As the first gleam of dawn pierced the mountain mist, awaking his disciples, they looked in wonder at their Master, for his face shone with unearthly radiance. In the mist the figures of Moses and Elijah, the prophets of old, seemed to rise before them. They heard a Voice—the Voice that Jesus had heard in Jordan—saying—'This is my beloved Son; hear ye him.' Peter, still confused with sleep, kindling with the marvel of what he saw, but hardly knowing what he was saying, cried: 'Rabbi, it is good for us to be here: and let us set up three tents: one for thee, one for Moses, and one for Elijah.'

A bright cloud swept across. The dazzled, awe-struck three fell on their faces. Jesus came and touched them on the shoulder. They looked up; the vision had disappeared; they saw no man, but Jesus only.

As they came down the mountain side, Jesus commanded the three that they should not tell even their fellow disciples the experience that they had shared until he himself should have suffered death and triumphed over it.

Approaching Caesarea Philippi, where they had left the nine other disciples, they saw a great crowd gathered round a group that was evidently having a fierce argument.

When Jesus came in sight some of them ran towards him.

'What question ye with them?' asked Jesus.

'Master,' replied one of them, 'I brought unto thee my son, which hath a dumb spirit; and wheresoever it taketh him, it dasheth him down: and he foameth and grindeth his teeth and pineth away: and I spake to thy disciples that they should cast it out; and they were not able.'

'O faithless generation,' Jesus sighed, 'how long shall I be with you? How long shall I bear with you? Bring him hither to me.'

The boy, evidently suffering from epilepsy, fell on the ground.

'How long time is it,' Jesus asked, 'since this hath come unto him?'

'From a child,' replied the father, 'for often he falleth into the fire and oft times into the water. If thou canst do anything, have compassion on us and help us.'

'If thou canst!' exclaimed Jesus. 'All things are possible to him that believeth.'

'I believe,' cried the father with all the intensity of his longing: 'help thou mine unbelief.'

By this time the whole multitude was surging towards Jesus and the man and his boy. So Jesus without more ado said:

'Thou dumb and deaf spirit, I command thee: come out of him and enter no more into him.'

The boy, with a shriek, writhed on the ground and then lay still.

'He is dead,' gasped the crowd.

Jesus, stooping, gripped the boy's hand and helped him to his feet. He was cured from that hour.

The Twelve went with Jesus to the house where they were staying. The nine were greatly troubled because they had failed to heal the boy themselves.

'Why could not we cast it out?'

'Because of your little faith,' Jesus replied. 'This kind can come out by nothing, save by prayer.'

After this they started towards home once more. As they walked Jesus tried again to accustom them to the thought that soon they would no longer have him at hand to teach them.

'The Son of Man,' he said, 'shall be delivered up into the hands of men and they shall kill him—the third day he shall be raised up.'

They were exceedingly grieved at this. For to them it seemed the end of all things. For the sake of Jesus they had left fishing-nets and boats, the customs-office, their homes. Now he was to be snatched from them.

When Jesus was walking ahead of them in thought they fell to disputing with one another. Each was boasting that he was the greatest of the Twelve. At last Capernaum and the familiar coast-line came into sight. They went into Peter's house. When they were there Jesus looked round at the group and said:

'What were ye reasoning on the way?'

They felt very sheepish at this question. They were silent. Jesus, who had gathered the trend of their talk as their voices rose in the argument, called Peter's little boy to him and took him in his arms.

'If any man would be first,' he said, 'he shall be last of all, and servant of all. Whosoever,' he continued, 'shall receive one of such little children in my name, receiveth me, and whosoever receiveth me, receiveth .not me, but him that sent me: for he that is least among you all, the same is great. And whosoever shall give to drink a cup of cold water only in the name of a disciple, verily, I say unto you, he shall in no wise lose his reward.'

'And whosoever shall cause one of these little ones to stumble,' Jesus continued with great sternness, 'it were better for him that a millstone were hanged about his neck and he were cast into the sea.'

CHAPTER XIV
HIS FACE TOWARDS JERUSALEM

JESUS' brothers had been carping at him for the things that he did, and saying that he had taken leave of his senses. They now started to criticize him for what he was not doing. They began to upbraid him for staying quietly to teach his men instead of going to the Feast of the Ingathering at Jerusalem, for which they themselves were about to start.

Autumn had come. The grape-harvest was in full swing. The terraced vineyards on the hill-sides were alive with boys and girls, men and women, gathering the precious bunches. Boys were up in the branches of the old grey fig-trees getting down the ripe fruit to dry in the sunshine. The olives were being gathered, to be crushed for their delicious oil.

Everybody was preparing at the same time for the happy feast in which they thanked God for harvest. It was also called the Feast of Tents (or Tabernacles) because they built tents or huts on the house-tops and in the fields, and lived there during the feast. Pilgrims thronged from all over the Empire to Jerusalem for this feast, which lasted for eight days.

'Depart hence,' Jesus' brothers said to him, 'and go into Judaea that thy disciples also may see the works that thou doest. For there is no man that doeth anything in secret and he himself seeketh to be known openly. If thou do these things, show thyself to the world.'

Jesus said: 'Go ye up unto this feast: I go not up yet unto this feast, for my time is not yet fully come.'

The brothers went. They found that the deeds and words of Jesus were being much debated.

'He is a good man,' said some. 'Nay, but he deceives the people,' said others.

Some three or four days of the feast were already over when Jesus, having started with the Twelve after the roads were clear of pilgrims, came quietly into the city. He began at once to teach in one of the great open courts of the Temple.

On the last night the thousand temple lamps, the hundreds of torches, were put out. Jesus went across, as his custom was at the feasts, to the Mount of Olives. Dawn came, and with the sunrise he returned to the Temple and went to the place called the Treasury, where a number of trumpet-shaped receivers stood ready for the pilgrims' offerings to be thrown in. The level rays of the rising sun shed a myriad times more light than all the bright illumination of the last night of the feast. Jesus used this as a parable for his talk with the pilgrims who gathered round him.

'I am the Light of the World,' he said; 'he that followeth me shall not walk in darkness, but shall have the light of life.'

At this the Pharisees attacked him for saying of himself what was not true. Jesus told them that he only spoke what his Father gave him. To some who stood by him and believed in him Jesus said:

'If you continue in my word, then are ye my disciples indeed; and ye shall know the truth and the truth shall make you free.'

This made some of the Jews angry.

'We are Abraham's children: we have never been in bondage. How sayest thou, "Ye shall be free?"'

Jesus, in reply, showed them that the worst slavery was the slavery of sin. Those who opposed him grew more and more angry as the argument went on. They began to call him names, said he was a 'Samaritan', that he was possessed by a devil, and at last were so furious with his blasphemy in saying that God was his Father, that they

seized stones to hurl them at him and slay him. The mass
of pilgrims swirled about Jesus and, lost among them, he
made his way out of the Temple and once more crossed to
the Mount of Olives.

A Sabbath day after this feast found Jesus with the
Twelve in Jerusalem. A blind youth sat at the side of the
street begging. A disciple, perhaps John, who had relatives in Jerusalem, knew that the boy was blind from birth,
and asked whether the youth was born blind because of
his parents' sin, or his own.

'Neither,' replied Jesus, 'but that the works of God
should be made clear in him.' Jesus then spat on the
ground, made mud of the saliva and the earth, and
rubbed some of it on the youth's eyes.

'Go,' he said, 'wash in the Pool of Siloam.'

The lad sped as swiftly as his blindness would let him
down the hill that leads to the Pool, where the sacred water
of the spring runs in from the long, winding tunnel, over
a thousand feet through the entire hill, hewn in the rock
many centuries before by King Hezekiah. This water has
always been held to be sacred, because it flows and then
ceases and flows again, as though, the people say, some
angel touched it.

To this sacred water the youth hurried. Reaching the
marble edge he knelt, and dipping his hands in the water
dashed it in his eyes. For the first time in all his life he
saw. For the first time he knew the flame of sunshine
dancing from moving water that reflected blue sky, the
swing of a red-brown tunic on a running boy, the cedars
of the Mount of Olives, the white majesty of the Temple.

Tingling with joy he ran up the hill home. 'I can see,'
he cried.

'Is not this he that sat and begged?' exclaimed the
astonished neighbours.

'This is he,' said some.

'He is like him,' said others.

'I *am* he,' said the youth.

'How were thine eyes opened?' inquired the neighbours.

'A man that is called Jesus made clay and anointed mine eyes and said unto me, "Go to the Pool of Siloam and wash"; and I went and washed, and I received my sight.'

'Where is he?' they inquired.

'I know not,' said the youth.

The event was so amazing that some of them took the boy and told the leaders of the Temple about his receiving his sight.

Again the question was asked: 'How did you receive your sight?'

The boy answered shortly: 'He put clay upon mine eyes, and I washed and do see.'

'This man is not of God,' said some of the Pharisees, 'because he keepeth not the Sabbath day.'

'How can a man that is a sinner,' demanded others of the Pharisees, 'do such miracles?'

They disagreed vigorously on this and turned to the youth:

'What sayest thou of him that hath opened thine eyes?'

'He is a prophet,' the boy answered.

Baffled, unable to believe in the event, they sent for the boy's parents.

'Is this your son, who ye say was born blind? How, then, doth he now see?' they asked.

The parents were afraid. They knew that the leaders among the Jews had now agreed that if any man said that he was a follower of Jesus, he was to be put out of the synagogue. So they gave an evasive answer.

'We know that this is our son, and that he was born blind,' they answered. 'But by what means he now seeth, we know not; or who hath opened his eyes, we know not. He is of age. Ask him. He shall speak for himself.'

To be 'of age' under Jewish law meant that he was thirteen years old or over, when a boy becomes responsible for his own actions.

Turning to the boy the Pharisee leaders said: 'Give God the praise. We know that this man is a sinner.'

'Whether he be a sinner or no, I know not,' the boy replied. 'One thing I know, that, whereas I was blind, now I see.'

The rabbis were so baffled that they stupidly asked the boy to repeat his story, hoping to find some way to attack Jesus.

'What did he to thee?' they asked again. 'How opened he thine eyes?'

The boy was now angry and impatient. 'I have told you already,' he said, 'and ye did not hear. Wherefore would ye hear it again? Will ye also be his disciples?'

This stung them into a rage.

'Thou art his disciple,' they snarled. 'We are Moses' disciples. As for this fellow, we know not whence he is.'

'Why, herein is a marvellous thing,' the youth exclaimed, 'that ye know not whence he is, and yet he hath opened mine eyes. Now we know that God heareth not sinners. . . . If this man were not of God he could do nothing.'

The insolence of this young upstart in daring to try to teach them made them boil with wrath.

'Thou wast altogether born in sins,' they cried, 'and dost thou teach us?'

So they not only drove him out of their midst, but cut his name out of the membership of the synagogue, which was a terrible disgrace. One of the Twelve who had followed this whole discussion, probably John, told his Master that the young fellow had been thrown out on account of his loyalty to Jesus. Jesus immediately went to get into touch with him. When they met, Jesus put to him the question:

'Dost thou believe on the Son of Man?'

'Who is he, Lord,' asked the youth, 'that I might believe on him.'

'Thou hast seen him, and it is he that talketh with thee.'

'Lord,' said the youth, casting himself down at Jesus' feet, 'I believe.'

'I am come into the world for judgement,' Jesus said to those around listening, 'that they which see not, might see, and that they which see be made blind.'

'Are we blind?' asked some of the Pharisees sarcastically.

'If you were blind,' he answered, 'you would have no sin. But now you say, "We see", your sin remains.'

They wrangled about this. 'Why listen to him?' said some. 'He is mad.'

'These are not the words of one that hath an evil spirit,' others argued. 'Can an evil spirit open the eyes of the blind?'

So Jesus after all left Jerusalem that autumn without being arrested. He went north again with the Twelve, but barely three months later, in early December of the same year, they started south again to Jerusalem, for the Feast of the Dedication of the Temple. They took the shorter route through Samaria. As the evening came on they reached a Samaritan village. A couple of the disciples went ahead. The headman came out and they asked for a night's lodging. He saw that these were of the detested race of Jews and that they were on the way to their capital, Jerusalem. He flatly refused to let them stay in the village.

The disciples were angry. Did they recall that just here in Samaria, the old scroll of the Kings told them, Elijah had called down fire from heaven on the king who spurned Jehovah? John and James, the 'Sons of Thunder', cried:

'Master, let us call down fire from heaven and burn them up.'

'Ye know not,' Jesus replied to them, 'what manner of spirit you are of.' It was strange that after having been so long with him they should not yet have known what the Kingdom of God meant. So they passed on from that village and soon came to another. There they were well received and given a roof over their heads against the winter weather. They turned eastward by the road that leads through a harsh ravine of shattered rock down to the Jordan Valley. Their way now lay on the edge of the Samaritans' country. They came to another village. Near it were ten men whose discoloured faces and arms showed them to have the terrible disease of leprosy.

Of these ten men nine were Jews, the tenth was a Samaritan. Exiled from their different villages, they were comrades because of their common illness. They had somehow got word that Jesus and his Twelve were on that caravan route. They therefore waited among the rocks some way from the road, for the leper was by the Law of Moses compelled to keep as much as a hundred feet from the ways where men went. As Jesus came in sight they lined themselves up and called to him:

'Jesus, Master,' they cried out, 'have pity on us.'

'Go,' he replied, 'and show yourselves to the priests.'

To their delighted amazement the scales dropped from their skin, which became clean and glowing with health. They hurried off to find priests so that they might be certified as clean, and able to go into their own homes again. One of them, however, suddenly glowed with another idea, that he must first turn and give thanks to the great healer who had given him new life. So he ran back down the road to Jesus, crying:

'Praise God; Praise God.' Reaching Jesus he threw himself at his feet, thanking him. Jesus looked at the man—he was a Samaritan! Then he looked at the Twelve.

'Were not all ten cleansed?' he said. 'But where are the

nine? Was there no other to return and give glory to God except this alien?'

Did the 'Sons of Thunder' see even more deeply how senseless and wicked they had been to judge a whole people and want to call down fire from heaven on a whole village for the truculence of one man? Thinking many things they went on their way. As they walked farther on in this journey towards the Feast of Dedication, they were joined from time to time by other pilgrims. One had made up his mind to follow Jesus as a disciple. Jesus knew that any man who did that must be prepared for hardship and danger; because the hate of Herod, the cold plotting of Caiaphas and Annas were closing in on him and his.

'The foxes,' replied Jesus, 'have their holes, the birds have their nests; but the Son of Man has not where to lay his head.'

Another enthusiastic pilgrim said: 'I will follow thee, Lord; but first suffer me to say farewell to my home.'

Again Jesus saw that the man's family would din into his ears how lunatic he must be to leave all and join a homeless wonder-worker.

'No one is worthy of the Kingdom of God,' he said, 'who, having put his hand to the plough, turns back.'

They saw the point of the little parable; for the winter fields were alive with men guiding their ploughs which, if they turned away their heads to look elsewhere, might strike a big stone or a piece of rock and break.

'Lord,' asked another who was eager to follow him, 'suffer me first to bury my father.'

This did not mean that the man's father was dead, but that the man wished to stay on in his father's home until his death, and that then he would follow him. Thus Jesus' reply, 'Let the dead bury their dead', was not a harsh one.

Discussions took place as they walked down the Jordan Valley towards Jericho. Many questions were asked about the Kingdom of God. One Pharisee asked a question that was in all their minds: 'When will the Kingdom of God come?'

'The Kingdom of God,' replied Jesus, 'cometh not with observation. Ye will not say, "Lo here"; or "Lo there". The Kingdom of God is within you.'

They now passed through Jericho to face the steep, rocky climb up the Judaean hills to Jerusalem.

'Master,' inquired a lawyer, perhaps more to test Jesus than to get new truth, 'what must I do to inherit eternal life?'

'What says the Law,' replied Jesus. 'How readest thou?'

'Thou shalt love the Lord thy God with all thy heart and with all thy soul, and with all thy strength and with all thy mind,' the Lawyer quoted, adding, 'and thy neighbour as thyself.'

'Thou hast truly answered,' said Jesus; 'do this and thou shalt live.'

Jesus himself had made no reply. This did not satisfy the lawyer, who asked: 'But who is my neighbour?' This was a very searching question. For in the Scroll of Leviticus, from which the lawyer had quoted, 'neighbour' means 'fellow citizen,' that is, a Jew. Yet not many inches down the manuscript the Law says: 'The foreigner who settles beside you must be treated like a native, and you must love him as you love yourself; for you were foreigners yourselves in the land of Egypt.'

So Jesus began his story:

'A certain man was going down from Jerusalem to Jericho; and he fell among robbers, which both stripped him and beat him, and departed, leaving him half dead. And by chance a certain priest was going down that way: and when he saw him, he passed by on the other side. And in like manner, a Levite also, when he came to the place, and saw him, passed by on the other side. But a certain Samaritan, as he journeyed, came where he was: and when he saw him, he was moved with compassion, and came to him, and bound up his wounds, pouring on them oil and wine; and he set him on his own beast, and brought him to an inn, and took care of him. And on the morrow he took out two pence, and gave them to the host, and said, "Take care of him; and whatsoever thou spendest more, I, when I come back again, will repay thee." '

'Which of these three,' Jesus finished by asking the lawyer, 'proved neighbour to him that fell among the robbers?'

'He that showed mercy on him,' replied the lawyer.

'Go, and do thou likewise,' replied Jesus.

As the lawyer went his way he had much to think about. In Jesus' story it was the men who prided themselves on being the very agents of the Law of Moses who broke its great rule, the love of the neighbour. And more startling still, it was the Samaritan, despised as having polluted Jewish blood, detested for his scorn of Jerusalem, who really obeyed the Law that is at the foundation of the Kingdom of God.

So the Twelve, with Jesus, pursued their way. They passed the Red Mountain, so called because of the murders by robbers on the road. It was with a quickened pace that they saw at last, on the outer slope of the Mount of Olives, the village of Bethany, less than a mile from Jerusalem, but remote from all its feverish rush.

A man named Lazarus and his two sisters, Martha and Mary, were friends of Jesus there. They welcomed him under the roof of their little home. Having no servants Martha began making special preparations for their guest. She grew flustered as she hurried to get everything ready for Jesus. Mary did not care much about the meal so long as she could sit and listen to what Jesus had to say to them. Martha was annoyed with her sister, and came to Jesus and said:

'Lord, dost thou not care that my sister leaves me to serve alone? Bid her help me.'

'Martha, Martha,' said Jesus to her, 'thou art anxious and troubled about many things: but one thing is needful: for Mary hath chosen the good part, which shall not be taken away from her.'

Jesus, knowing what trouble lay ahead, felt that simple food set down without fuss was best, because it did not interfere with the quiet talk he wanted to have with them.

The next morning Jesus went by the winding road over the dip in the ridge of the Mount of Olives which is called 'the Bottle of the Winds'. The Feast of the Dedication came close to the time of what is now the Western Christmas, when the bitterly cold winds and heavy rain drive across the city. Jesus went into the Temple, and in the shelter of the great roofed-in court, called Solomon's Porch, the Twelve gathered round him and an increasing crowd of pilgrims, while he taught them.

The perplexity of the Sanhedrin was great. Many people believed that Jesus was the Christ. Even one member of the Sanhedrin, secretly believing this, had plucked up sufficient courage to demand a fair hearing for him. They gathered round him, asking a question that on the one side showed their perplexity, but on the other their cunning. For they would not really believe him if he said that he was the Christ; what they would do was to lay a charge against him at one and the same time of blasphemy and of rebellion against Rome—blasphemy in claiming to be the Son of God; rebellion in claiming as Messiah to be God's anointed ruler, in a land governed by Rome.

'How long dost thou make us to doubt? If thou art the Christ, tell us plainly.'

'I told you,' Jesus answered, 'and ye believed not. The things that I do in my Father's name, they bear witness of me.'

This straight answer did not give them the handle against him that they desired. As he looked from the crafty faces of these leaders to the crowd of pilgrims, Ezekiel's picture of the lazy shepherds battening on their flock came back to Jesus. With it he recalled how, as a boy, he had seen the Nazareth shepherd lead his flocks to good pasture; to water-springs by day and to the safety of the fold by night— that fold with the hole in the wall in which the shepherd rolled himself at night so that his body protected the sheep from the wolf, even if he had to fight to the death. Nay, the shepherd might even have to give his life for the sheep, fighting the robber who came climbing over the wall.

'Verily, verily, I say unto you, he that entereth not by the door into the fold of the sheep, but climbeth up some other way, the same is a thief and a robber. But he that entereth in by the door is the shepherd of the sheep. To him the porter openeth; and the sheep hear his voice: and he calleth his own sheep by name, and leadeth them out. When he hath put forth all his own, he goeth before them, and the sheep follow him: for they know his voice. And a stranger will they not follow, but will flee from him: for they know not the voice of strangers.'

As a picture this was clear as crystal to his hearers: they saw that happening every day; but what had it to do with Jesus and themselves? So he went on:

'Verily, verily, I say unto you, I am the door of the sheep. All that came before me are thieves and robbers: but the sheep did not hear them. I am the door: by me if any man enter in, he shall be saved, and shall go in and out, and shall find pasture. The thief cometh not, but that he may steal, and kill and destroy: I came that they may have life, and may have it abundantly. I am the good shepherd: the good shepherd layeth down his life for the sheep. He that is a hireling, and not a shepherd, whose own the sheep are not, beholdeth the wolf coming, and leaveth the sheep, and fleeth, and the wolf snatcheth them, and scattereth them: he fleeth because he is a hireling, and careth not for the sheep. I am the good shepherd; and I know mine own, and mine own know me, even as the Father knoweth me, and I know the Father; and I lay down my life for the sheep. And other sheep I have, which are not of this fold: them also I must bring, and they shall hear my voice; and they shall become one flock, and one shepherd. Therefore doth the Father love me, because I lay down my life, that I may take it again. No one taketh it away from me, but

The shepherd and his sheep

I lay it down of myself. I have power to lay it down, and I have power to take it again. This commandment received I from my Father.'

'I and my Father are one,' he concluded.

To the pilgrims it was truth; to the leaders from the Sanhedrin it was wicked blasphemy. And the punishment for blasphemy under the Law of Moses was that a man should be stoned to death. They seized stones to do this. Jesus faced them.

'Many good works have I showed you from my Father,' he said. 'For which of these works do ye stone me?'

'For a good work we stone thee not,' they stormed, 'but for blasphemy: and because that thou, being a man, makest thyself God.'

'If I do not the works of my Father, believe me not. But if I do them, though ye believe not me, believe the works: that ye may know and understand that the Father is in me, and I in the Father.'

Again they made at him to arrest him. But amongst the crowd of pilgrims who believed in him he escaped. The second attempted arrest had failed. Jesus was determined that not till the great feast of the whole year, that of the Passover, should the final test come. Making his way out of the city with the Twelve he took farewell of his Bethany friends on the slope of the Mount of Olives and went eastward down the Jericho road, and so up the Jordan Valley to the ford where John had baptized him. There, in the place where the clear Voice of God had spoken in him, saying, 'Thou art my Son, the Beloved', he taught his men and faced the struggle that was bound to break upon him within a few months in the spring at the Passover. But he was to go up those hills sooner than he had expected. A man came all hot and tired with travel to call Jesus to go up with all speed to Bethany.

'Martha and Mary have sent me,' he said, 'with this message, "Lord, behold, he whom thou lovest is sick." '

Jesus loved Martha and her sister and Lazarus; yet he

waited two days before starting to help them. His disciples warned him against going at all.

'Master,' they pleaded, 'the leaders sought recently to stone-thee: goest thou thither again?'

'Are there not twelve hours in the day,' answered Jesus, using a common proverb of the people that a man would not die till his hour had come. 'I go to awaken our friend Lazarus who is sleeping. He is dead,' Jesus went on; 'nevertheless, let us go to him.'

Even the Twelve flinched at the idea of walking straight into the jaws of death at the hands of the Sanhedrin. With the courage of a man who faces hard facts, but will not fail his leader, Thomas the Twin cried to the others: 'Let us also go, that we may die with him.'

Once more they toiled up the steep, rocky way to Jerusalem, till they came round the last bend to the little town of Bethany. He did not want to break in on the grief of the sisters: so he waited there.

A number of folk from Jerusalem had come out to comfort the sisters. Martha, as soon as she heard of his coming, hurried out. Mary could not steel herself for the effort. When Martha came to where Jesus was she said, with a shadow of reproach in her sorrow: 'Lord, if thou hadst been here my brother had not died.'

'Thy brother,' Jesus answered, 'shall rise again.'

'I know,' she said, 'that he shall rise again at the resurrection of the last day.'

'I am the resurrection and the life,' said Jesus. 'He that believeth in me, though he were dead, yet shall he live. Whosoever liveth and believeth in me, though he die, yet shall he live. Dost thou believe this?'

'Yea, Lord,' she answered, 'I believe that thou art the Christ, the Son of God, which should come into the world.'

So saying, Martha turned and went home. She took

her sister Mary aside from her mourning friends and whispered: 'The Master is come and calleth for thee.'

Mary rose and started out. The friends who had not heard what Martha said thought that she was going to the grave to weep. Going to where Jesus sat she said just what Martha had said, that her brother would not have died had he been there. Then she broke down again and sobbed. Jesus was so troubled in spirit that he wept. He asked them to lead him to the grave, a shallow cave cut in the hill-side with a stone shelf for the body and a circular stone rolled against the entrance. At Jesus' command men heaved at this stone and rolled it away. Jesus, praying for a moment in silence to God, then called out loudly: 'Lazarus, come forth.'

Bound though he was hand and foot, and with his face swathed, he hobbled out.

'Loose him,' said Jesus; 'let him go.'

Many Jews who so far had not believed in Jesus, now became followers of him. But when the news of this wonderful deed came to Caiaphas and his father-in-law, Annas, it worked no change of mind in them. Their purpose to kill him was only strengthened. Caiaphas hastily summoned the Sanhedrin.

'What do we?' they asked one another. 'For this man doeth many miracles. If we let him alone, all will believe on him; and the Romans will come and take away our status and destroy our nation.'

'Ye know nothing at all,' broke in Caiaphas, as president. 'Ye do not realize that it is expedient for us that one man should die for the people, and that the whole nation perish not.' There were to be no more divided counsels; it was decided to plot steadily to achieve the death of Jesus. Their hope was to get him out of the way quietly when no pilgrims were there to raise a riot. Jesus, however, had decided to face the issue at his time, not theirs. So he rapidly set out with the Twelve north-eastward from Jerusalem over little-frequented tracks that skirt the Wilderness of Beth-aven. There in a tiny town called Ephraim, that looked eastward down the steep ways into the Jordan Valley, Jesus continued to teach the Twelve.

He did not stay there long. Some weeks still stretched between him and the date of the Passover in Jerusalem. At Ephraim, facing him across the Jordan Valley, was the land of Transjordania, with its League of Ten Greek Cities—Decapolis. He decided to go through that land by a circular route with his men, and from it to make his way to the Holy City. It was far beyond the reach either of Herod or of Caiaphas. He started thither in company with the Twelve and with some of their relatives. Salome, the mother of James and John, was one of these.

Crossing the Jordan, they went up the valley of the Yarmuk river that sings its way over boulders and rapids down to the quiet Jordan. Climbing that valley till they were at least three thousand feet above the Jordan, they walked over the rolling lands of 'Healthy Palestine', as the Romans called Transjordania.

One Sabbath a Pharisee invited Jesus to be his guest. A man, ill with dropsy, came into the courtyard. Instantly the question leapt to the minds of the Pharisees and lawyers, who were Jesus' fellow guests: 'Would Jesus dare to break the Sabbath by healing him?'

'Is it right', asked Jesus, 'to heal on the Sabbath, or is it not?'

Brave, honest men would either have said: 'No, the Tradition of the Elders says we must not,' or, 'Yes; surely it is God's will that he be made whole.' But they took refuge in cowardly silence. Calling the man to him, Jesus laid hands on him and sent him away cured and happy. He then asked them a question that left them as dumb as before.

'Which of you, if his son or his ox fall into the water-tank on the Sabbath, will not pull him out?'

At this dinner some of the guests had taken the best places. Jesus said to them:

'When thou art bidden of any man to a marriage feast, sit not down in the chief seat; lest haply a more honourable man than thou be bidden of him, and he that bade thee and him shall come and say to thee, "Give this man place"; and then thou shalt begin with shame to take the lowest place. But when thou art bidden go and sit down in the lowest place; that when he that hath bidden thee cometh, he may say to thee, "Friend, go up higher"; thou shalt then have glory in the presence of all that sit at meat with thee. For every one that exalteth himself shall be humbled; and he that humbleth himself shall be exalted.'

On hearing Jesus say this a guest ejaculated: 'Blessed is he that shall eat bread in the Kingdom of God.' Jesus told a story arising out of this remark:

'A certain man made a great supper; and he bade many: and he sent forth his servant at supper time to say to them that were bidden, "Come, for all things are now ready." And they with one consent began to make excuse. The first said unto him, "I have bought a field, and I must needs go out and see it: I pray thee have me excused." And another said, "I have bought five yoke of oxen, and I go to prove them: I pray thee have me excused." And another said, "I have married a wife, and therefore cannot come." And the servant came, and told his lord these things. Then the master of the house, being angry, said to his servant, "Go out quickly into the streets and lanes of the city, and bring in hither the poor and maimed and blind and lame." And the servant said, "Lord, what thou didst command is done, and yet there is room." And the lord said unto the servant, "Go out into the highways and hedges, and constrain them to come in, that my house may be filled. For I say unto you, that none of those men which were bidden shall taste of my supper."'

At just such another dinner the Pharisees criticized Jesus for sitting down without first having his hands and wrists rinsed in water by a servant.

'How do ye Pharisees cleanse the outside of the cup and plate,' he exclaimed, 'but within ye are full of craft and wickedness. Woe to you, Pharisees; ye give a tenth of mint and rue and every herb, but you have left undone justice and mercy and faith. But these ought ye to have done and not left the other undone. Ye love the best places at feasts, the chief seats in the synagogues and to be saluted in the market places. Woe to you! Ye are like graves whited over, outwardly beautiful, but inwardly dead men's bones.'

A lawyer reproved him, saying: 'Master, in saying this thou reproachest us also.'

'Yes,' he replied, 'woe to you lawyers also! Ye lay on men burdens grievous to be borne and ye yourselves touch not the burdens with one of your fingers. Ye build the tombs of the prophets—and your fathers killed them. Ye take away the key of knowledge: ye shut the Kingdom of Heaven from men; ye enter not in yourselves, and them that would enter ye prevent.'

He warned the people against the spirit of the Pharisees. But they were not to be afraid of them, even although they could have men put to death.

'I say unto you, my friends; be not afraid of them which kill the body, but are not able to kill the soul: but rather fear him which is able to destroy both soul and body.'

As another reason for bravely facing death, as he himself was now to do, he said: 'Are not five sparrows sold for two farthings? And not one of them is forgotten in the sight of God. For the very hairs of your head are all numbered. Fear not: ye are of more value than many sparrows.'

One in the crowd—a man whose father had just died and who was quarrelling with his brother about the property—broke in with a selfish request.

'Master,' he said, 'bid my brother divide the inheritance with me.'

'Man,' answered Jesus, 'who made me a judge or a

divider over you?' Then he went to the very root of the
trouble between the man and his brother.

'Take heed and keep yourselves from covetousness: for
a man's life consisteth not in the abundance of the things
which he possesseth.'

Jesus went on to tell a story that must surely have come
out of something that he had seen as a boy in his father's
workshop.

'The ground of a certain rich man brought forth plentifully: and
he reasoned within himself, saying, "What shall I do, because I have
not where to bestow my fruits?" And he said, "This will I do: I will
pull down my barns, and build greater; and there will I bestow all
my corn and my goods. And I will say to my soul, 'Soul, thou hast
much goods laid up for many years; take thine ease, eat, drink, be
merry.'" But God said unto him, "Thou foolish one, this night is thy
soul required of thee; and the things which thou hast prepared, whose
shall they be?" So is he that layeth up treasure for himself, and is
not rich toward God.'

Turning to his own men, Jesus went on to repeat to
them what he had said on the mountain by the Lake—
something easy enough to understand, but so difficult to
carry out that it needs to be said again and again—that
men should not be anxious what they are to eat and drink.

'For all these things do the nations of the world seek
after: but your Father knoweth that ye have need of these
things. Howbeit, seek ye His Kingdom and these things
shall be added unto you.'

He summed it up in a little parable from his own home-
life of the chest made by Joseph for the clothes of the family.

'Fear not, little flock; for it is your Father's good pleasure
to give you the Kingdom. Sell that ye have and give alms.
Make for yourselves purses which wax not old, a treasure
in the heavens that faileth not, where no thief draweth
near, neither moth destroyeth. For wherever your treasure
is, there will your heart be also.'

Many things he said to them, mostly in parables that

had a deep meaning, but because they were stories they stayed in the memory of all those who heard them. For instance, he told a story to illustrate the patience of God with men, but showing, too, that in the end men would be judged according to their deeds.

'A certain man had a fig tree planted in his vineyard; and he came seeking fruit thereon, and found none. And he said unto the vine-dresser, "Behold, these three years I come seeking fruit on this fig tree, and find none: cut it down; why doth it also cumber the ground?" And he answering saith unto him, "Lord, let it alone this year also, till I shall dig about it, and dung it; and if it bear fruit thenceforth, well; but if not, thou shalt cut it down." '

Jesus now continued his journey southward through Transjordania in order to reach Jerusalem by the Passover Feast. He again, as he looked forward to the time of testing that lay ahead, warned those who would follow him to count the cost.

'For which of you, desiring to build a tower, doth not first sit down and count the cost, whether he have wherewith to complete it? Lest haply, when he hath laid a foundation, and is not able to finish, all that behold begin to mock him, saying, "This man began to build, and was not able to finish." Or what king, as he goeth to encounter another king in war, will not sit down first and take counsel whether he is able with ten thousand to meet him that cometh against him with twenty thousand? Or else, while the other is yet a great way off, he sendeth an ambassage, and asketh conditions of peace. So therefore whosoever he be of you that renounceth not all that he hath, he cannot be my disciple.'

Pressing close around Jesus as he talked were publicans and sinners, anxious to be better men and women. Jesus took meals with them. The Pharisees and the Scribes were bitterly critical. They said: 'This man receiveth sinners and eateth with them.'

Jesus turned and asked two questions: first, one to the men and then one to the women.

The question to the men was:

'What man of you, having a hundred sheep, and having lost one of them, doth not leave the ninety and nine in the wilderness, and go after that which is lost, until he find it? And when he hath found it, he layeth it on his shoulders, rejoicing. And when he cometh home, he calleth together his friends and his neighbours, saying unto them, "Rejoice with me, for I have found my sheep which was lost." I say unto you, that even so there shall be joy in heaven over one sinner that repenteth, more than over ninety and nine righteous persons, which need no repentance.'

The question to the women was:

'Or what woman having ten pieces of silver, if she lose one piece, doth not light a lamp, and sweep the house, and seek diligently until she find it? And when she hath found it, she calleth together her friends and neighbours, saying, "Rejoice with me, for I have found the piece which I lost." Even so, I say unto you, there is joy in the presence of the angels of God over one sinner that repenteth.'

Then Jesus went on to tell one of the loveliest of his stories, the one we call the Parable of the Prodigal Son. He said:

'A certain man had two sons: and the younger of them said to his father, "Father, give me the portion of thy substance that falleth to me." And he divided unto them his living. And not many days after the younger son gathered all together, and took his journey into a far country; and there he wasted his substance with riotous living. And when he had spent all, there arose a mighty famine in that country; and he began to be in want. And he went and joined himself to one of the citizens of that country; and he sent him into his fields to feed swine. And he would fain have been filled with the husks that the swine did eat: and no man gave unto him. But when he came to himself he said, "How many hired servants of my father's have bread enough and to spare, and I perish here with hunger! I will arise and go to my father, and will say unto him, 'Father, I have sinned against heaven, and in thy sight: I am no more worthy to be called thy son: make me as one of thy hired servants'." And he arose, and came to his father. But while he was yet afar off, his father saw him, and was moved with compassion, and ran, and fell on his neck, and kissed him. And the son said unto him, "Father, I have sinned against heaven, and in thy sight; I am no more worthy to be called thy son." But the father said to his servants, "Bring forth quickly the best robe, and put it on him; and put a ring on his hand, and shoes on his feet: and bring the fatted calf, and kill it, and let us eat, and make merry; for this my son was dead and is alive again; he was lost, and is found." And they began to be merry. Now his elder son was in the field: and as he came and drew nigh to the house, he heard music and dancing. And he called to him one of the servants, and inquired what these things might be. And he said unto him, "Thy brother is come; and thy father hath killed the fatted calf, because he hath received him safe and sound." But he was angry, and would not go in: and his father came out, and intreated him. But he answered and said to his father, "Lo, these many years do I serve thee, and I never transgressed a commandment of thine: and yet thou never gavest me a kid, that I might make merry with my friends: but when this thy son came, which hath devoured thy living with harlots, thou killedst for him the fatted calf." And he said unto him, "Son, thou art ever with me, and all that is mine is thine. But it was meet to make merry and be glad: for this thy brother was dead, and is alive again; and was lost, and is found." '

The Twelve and those with them were now led by Jesus to a small city perched on steep, rocky hill-sides. It was the last town at which they would rest before crossing the Jordan Valley to Jericho and Jerusalem. In this place Jesus again spoke against the people who thought themselves to be better than others.

'Two men went up into the temple to pray; the one a Pharisee, and the other a publican. The Pharisee stood and prayed thus with himself, "God, I thank thee, that I am not as the rest of men, extortioners, unjust, adulterers, or even as this publican. I fast twice in the week; I give tithes of all that I get." But the publican, standing afar off, would not lift up so much as his eyes unto heaven, but smote his breast, saying, "God, be merciful to me a sinner." I say unto you, This man went down to his house justified rather than the other: for every one that exalteth himself shall be humbled; but he that humbleth himself shall be exalted.'

Some small children were in their mothers' arms as the women stood close by listening to Jesus' words. These mothers wished that a rabbi so good and loving and wise as Jesus might bless their children. They agreed to ask him. They gathered up their courage and began to come towards him in a group, carrying the tiny ones and leading the others by the hand. As some of the disciples saw this they bustled up to them, and asked what they wanted. They explained that they wished the Master to bless their children. Roughly, the disciples refused and began to drive the mothers back, while the babies whimpered at the stern faces of the disciples. How could Jesus on his way to face the great crisis at Jerusalem stop for anything so unimportant as blessing babies.

Jesus saw what they were doing. He was indignant.

'Suffer the little children to come unto me,' he cried, stretching out his arms to them, 'and forbid them not: for of such is the Kingdom of Heaven. Verily, I say unto you, Whosoever shall not receive the Kingdom of God as a little child, he shall in no wise enter therein.'

He smiled into the smiling faces of wondering boys and girls as he took them in his arms and blessed them, laying his hands upon them.

Listening and watching was a young sheikh who owned much land and many cattle and sheep. Very rich, he could command whatsoever he wished; and he loved wealth and power. But he was hungry for something greater still. He saw it in Jesus. So, as Jesus said 'Goodbye' to the children and their mothers, and moved away on his journey towards Jerusalem, the young man seized this opportunity of questioning Jesus.

Jesus was already on the march. The rich young ruler ran to catch up with him. Then he bowed down in the dust of the road.

'Good Master,' he cried, 'what good thing shall I do that I may have eternal life?'

'Why callest thou me "Good"?' exclaimed Jesus. 'None is good, save one, God. Thou knowest the commandments, "Do not kill, Do not steal, Honour thy father and mother."'

'All these things have I observed from my youth. What lack I yet?' cried the youth.

Jesus, as he looked at the young man, loved him. He

longed to have him in the company going on to face death
in Jerusalem, to see him wholly given to the Kingdom of
God—young, with keen brain and high ideals, vigorous,
accustomed to command. But anything short of complete
giving of himself would mean tragic failure under the test
ahead of them. Jesus pierced straight to the young sheikh's
weak point and made that the test. The youth had said
'What lack I yet?' Jesus told him.

'If thou wouldst be perfect, go, sell that thou hast, and
give to the poor, and thou shalt have treasure in heaven,
and come, follow me.'

The young man's face fell: he turned away and went
back to his slaves. Jesus was as sorrowful as was the young
man. He looked round at the wondering faces of his
Twelve who had given up their all for him, and exclaimed:
'How hardly shall they that have riches enter into the
Kingdom of God.'

The Twelve were amazed at these words.

'Children,' he repeated, 'how hard it is for them that
trust in riches to enter into the Kingdom of God. It is
easier for a camel to go through a needle's eye than for
a rich man to enter into the Kingdom of God.'

'Then who can be saved?' they demanded.

'With man it is impossible,' Jesus replied, looking
earnestly into their faces, 'but not with God: for all things
are possible with God.'

'Lo, we have left all,' said Peter, 'and have followed
thee; what then shall we have?'

'Verily, I say unto you,' Jesus replied, 'that there is no
man that hath left house, or brethren or sister or mother
or father or children or lands for my sake, and for the
gospel's, but shall receive a hundredfold, and shall (as the
young ruler had asked) inherit eternal life.'

'Many that are first shall be last,' he concluded, 'and the
last first.'

This saying led Jesus to illustrate what he meant by a parable that has perplexed many. It is a story about unemployed workmen at the busy season in the vineyards.

'The kingdom of heaven is like unto a man that is a householder, which went out early in the morning to hire labourers into his vineyard. And when he had agreed with the labourers for a penny a day, he sent them into his vineyard. And he went out about the third hour, and saw others standing in the market-place idle; and to them he said, "Go ye also into the vineyard, and whatsoever is right I will give you." And they went their way. Again he went out about the sixth and the ninth hour, and did likewise. And about the eleventh hour he went out, and found others standing; and he saith unto them, "Why stand ye here all the day idle?" They say unto him, "Because no man hath hired us." He saith unto them, "Go ye also into the vineyard." And when even was come, the lord of the vineyard saith unto his steward, "Call the labourers, and pay them their hire, beginning from the last unto the first." And when they came that were hired about the eleventh hour, they received every man a penny. And when the first came, they supposed that they would receive more; and they likewise received every man a penny. And when they received it, they murmured against the householder, saying, "These last have spent but one hour, and thou hast made them equal unto us, which have borne the burden of the day and the scorching heat." But he answered and said to one of them, "Friend, I do thee no wrong: didst not thou agree with me for a penny? Take up that which is thine, and go thy way: it is my will to give unto this last, even as unto thee. Is it not lawful for me to do what I will with mine own? or is thine eye evil, because I am good?" So the last shall be first, and the first last.'

We grasp the meaning of this strange story more strongly if we recall that Peter had followed up his statement, 'We have left all', with the question: 'What shall we get?' God, Jesus shows, does not want men to measure the service that they give to him by what they can get out of it. They should serve him as a Father for love. God opens the door of His Kingdom; and if you are in the Kingdom, you are in it: that is the equal wage for all. As the father said in the parable, 'All that I have is yours.' The son could not wish more for himself, or less for any one else.

As they went on down the winding valleys, into the broad, low Jordan rift, Jesus walked often ahead of the Twelve thinking out what lay before him. So concentrated was his thought that the Twelve whispered to one another in awe. They felt that the Kingdom was, indeed, at hand. But what did it mean for them? In spite of all that he had said of leaven working silently and of quiet growth of seed, and of its being a Kingdom of the spirit of a child, the old idea still had its hold on their minds: Jesus overturning the existing rule of the Romans, and in the power of God setting up the throne of David in Jerusalem. What glory for the Twelve! To be the King's Counsellors.

Salome, the wife of Zebedee who was at home fishing and mending the nets, was burning with ambition for her sons, James and John. She would try to get them the highest seats of authority in the land. She bided her time and then, without letting any of the other disciples know, she chose a quiet moment when Jesus was alone and sped to him with her sons: 'I wish to ask something,' she said.

'What wouldest thou?' he asked.

'Command that these my two sons may sit, one on thy right hand and one on thy left hand in thy Kingdom.'

'Ye know not what ye ask,' he answered; and, turning to the youths. 'Are ye able to drink the cup that I am about to drink?'

'We are able,' they exclaimed eagerly in their blindness.

'My cup, indeed, ye shall drink:' Jesus answered gently, 'but to sit on my right hand and on my left hand is not mine to give, but it is for them for whom it hath been prepared by my Father.'

The ten were angry when they heard that their fellow disciples had tried, on the sly, to bespeak the positions of principal Ministers of State. Jesus called the stormy Twelve to him. All, and especially the 'Sons of Thunder', looked shamefaced.

'Ye know,' said Jesus, 'that the rulers of the other nations lord it over them, and their great men exercise authority over them. They that have authority over them,' he said with a flash of sarcasm, 'are called "Benefactors". He that would become "great" among you shall be your servant, and he who would be the greatest shall be the servant of all; even as the Son of Man came not to be served, but to serve and to give his life a ransom for many.'

The disciples would see the meaning very clearly. For 'Benefactor' was the name that the ruler of Egypt gave himself in those days; and 'greatest' (Maximus) was the title of the Emperor at Rome; while a 'ransom' was the price a Roman would pay to buy freedom for a slave.

Jesus led his little company on across the Jordan Valley. Lonely he must have felt because even now they had not really grasped what his Kingdom meant. They waded the ford of the river and followed the camel-caravan tracks across the dried mud of spring-time left by the 'swelling of Jordan' in the February floods.

'We go up to Jerusalem,' he said, 'and the Son of Man shall be given up to the chief priests and scribes: and they shall condemn him to death and deliver him to the Romans; to mock and scourge and crucify—and after three days, he shall be raised up.'

Through the hot, steamy atmosphere of the valley, so different from the bracing breezes of the Transjordania, that they had just left, they moved on to the great city that loomed ahead—Jericho. Its ruler now was Pontius Pilate. Herod the Great had built its superb amphitheatre and a marble palace for himself, which his son, Prince Archelaus, had rebuilt when the rebellious Jews had burned it down after Herod the Great's death. Beyond Jericho towered the hills that they must climb to Jerusalem.

Jericho at the south end of the Jordan Valley, like

Capernaum at the north end, was at the meeting of the ways from north and south, east and west. At this centre tens of thousands of pilgrims met, before breasting the last steep twenty-mile climb to Jerusalem. Already the rumour of Jesus' coming had run through the crowds. Many believed that he would bring in the Kingdom; thousands more were intensely curious to see him and to discover if this were, indeed, true.

No one in all Jericho was more eager to see Jesus than its most hated citizen, a man who had grown wealthy as chief inspector of taxes. He farmed out to lesser officials the right to collect the taxes, with the result that the people were forced to pay larger sums than were justly due. His name was Zacchaeus. Zacchaeus had certainly heard that the Pharisees twitted Jesus with being, as they said, 'the friend of publicans and sinners'. But the news had spread among the tax-collectors all up and down the Jordan Valley, that one of their colleagues, Matthew, at the great customs barrier in Capernaum, had given up his position, with all its opportunities of making money, and that he had become a disciple of Jesus.

Zacchaeus was curious to see the Teacher who had had such an extraordinary influence on a tax-gatherer. As he was a short man, he nimbly got ahead of the crowd and hoisted himself up among the leaves of a wayside sycamore tree. The crowd came along, Jesus leading the way. They were passing his tree. No—they had stopped! Jesus was calling his name!

'Zacchaeus, make haste and come down; for to-day I must abide at thy house.'

Zacchaeus almost tumbled out of the tree in his haste to take Jesus to his home. Jesus had both given Zacchaeus his friendship and asked him for the courtesies of a host.

Jesus had done a daring act. For, just as he was going to face the hate of the high priest and his followers, against which his sole bulwark was his popularity with the pilgrims, he deliberately braved their anger.

'He is to lodge with a man that is a sinner,' they all murmured.

'Behold, Lord,' said Zacchaeus, 'the half of my riches I give to the poor; and if I have wrongfully exacted aught of any man, I restore it fourfold.'

Jesus' heart was thrilled with joy. The Parables of the Lost Sheep, the Lost Coin, the Prodigal Son came true in one man. Zacchaeus had without being asked accepted the test that only a few days ago sent the rich young ruler away sorrowful.

Jesus delayed entering Zacchaeus' house in order to tell the multitude a story. He told it because they were expecting the Kingdom of God to come at once, a Kingdom with a throne in Jerusalem. Supposing that within two or three days the pilgrim Jews in Jerusalem suddenly caught fire with this patriotic enthusiasm for a Jewish national kingdom, and that fire were blown to white heat by religious passion in the belief that he himself was the Messiah, Jesus might find himself acclaimed King by half a million Jews in defiance of the rule of Rome. This would bring them all to disaster. To cool their heads and give them clearer vision, he told them this story. It gripped them from the outset, for it was based on a true story they all knew.

'A certain nobleman went into a far country to receive for himself a kingdom and to return.'

All heads would nod at this, for that is what Herod the Great's elder son, Prince Archelaus, who had lived at Jericho, did on his father's death. He went to the Emperor Augustus to ask that he might reign over Judaea. This lord wanted to discover which of his servants were best fitted to be chosen as provincial governors on his return.

'He called ten servants of his,' Jesus continued, 'and he gave them ten pounds, and said to them "Trade ye herewith till I come." But his citizens hated him and sent messengers after him, saying "We will not that this man reign over us!" '

'And it came to pass', Jesus went on, 'when he was come back again, having received the kingdom, that he commanded these servants, unto whom he had given the money, to be called to him, that he might know what they had gained by trading. And the first came before him, saying, "Lord, thy pound hath made ten pounds more." And he said unto him, "Well done, thou good servant: because thou wast found faithful in a very little, have thou authority over ten cities." And the second came, saying, "Thy pound, Lord, hath made five pounds." And he said to him also, "Be thou also over five cities." And another came, saying, "Lord, behold, here is thy pound, which I kept laid up in a napkin: for I feared thee, because thou art an austere man: thou takest up that thou layedst not down, and reapest that thou didst not sow". He saith unto him, "Out of thine own mouth will I judge thee, thou wicked servant. Thou knewest that I am an austere man, taking up what I laid not down, and reaping that I did not sow; then wherefore gavest thou not my money into the bank, and I at my coming should have required it with interest?" And he said unto them that stood by, "Take away from him the pound and give it unto him that hath the ten pounds." And they said unto him, "Lord, he hath ten pounds." "I say unto you, that unto every one that hath shall be given; but from him that hath not, even that which he hath shall be taken away from him. Howbeit these mine enemies, which would not that I reign over them, bring hither, and slay them before me." '

This was a true story, for Archelaus on coming back had rewarded faithful servants with governorships and had terribly revenged himself on those who plotted against him. The story aimed at showing the people the same truth that Jesus had tried to make his disciples see in the story of the labourers and the vineyard, that we must not serve God for what we can get out of our service, whether as a person or as a nation. We must do for Him all we can; and our reward is not to have an easy time, but to shoulder with joy greater responsibility.

It was now the eve of the Sabbath. Jesus rested through

that day with Zacchaeus. On the first day of the week, only one week before the Passover, which that year fell on the Sabbath, he started out to walk to Jerusalem. Thousands of other pilgrims were on the march. When they were leaving Jericho, a blind man, Bar-Timaeus, or Son of Timaeus, hearing the feet of a multitude on the way, asked what was happening.

'Jesus of Nazareth is passing by,' they told him.

Bar-Timaeus raised his voice and shouted as loud as he could: 'Jesus, thou Son of David, have mercy on me.'

'Hold your peace,' shouted many at him.

But he cried out all the more: 'Thou Son of David, have mercy on me.'

'Call ye him,' said Jesus, standing and waiting.

'Be of good cheer. Rise, he calleth thee,' said the crowd to Bar-Timaeus.

So eager was he that he threw away his cloak, sprang up, and hurried to Jesus.

'What wilt thou that I should do unto thee?' asked Jesus.

'Rabboni,' he replied, using a word of deep reverence, 'that I may receive my sight.'

'Go thy way,' said Jesus; 'thy faith hath made thee whole.'

The man jumped for joy; he could see. He shouted the praises of God, as did the multitude. But he did not go his way. He followed Jesus to Jerusalem. All day they continued the ascent. It was a walk of twenty miles and more, and a climb of some three thousand feet.

That day, while they climbed the steep ascent, old Annas, his son-in-law Caiaphas, with the Sanhedrin, discussed what to do if and when Jesus should reach Jerusalem. They were to be told where he lodged; and they could then take steps to arrest him. Before nightfall they were—as we shall see—to receive such a shock as they little expected.

Jesus himself had already made up his mind to act first and to bring the crisis to a head at once by boldly entering Jerusalem as Messiah. The words of the prophet Zechariah, words that every Jew knew by heart, sang in his heart as he walked:

> 'Rejoice, greatly, O daughter of Zion;
> Shout, O daughter of Jerusalem:
> Behold thy King cometh unto thee:
> He is just and having salvation.
> Lowly he comes, riding upon an ass,
> Even upon a colt, the foal of an ass.' [1]

The hour had come.

Quietly he sent a man ahead to ask a friend living on the Mount of Olives, in a village called Bethphage, to lend him his donkey. With the afternoon sun shining in their faces, Jesus, the Twelve, and the multitude of pilgrims came round the bend in the road that brought them on to the eastern slope of the Mount of Olives on the edge of Bethany village. Higher up the slope to the right the walls of Bethphage could be seen. Pointing in that direction, Jesus called two of the disciples and said:

'Go your way into the village that is over against you: and straightway, as ye enter it, ye shall find an ass tied and a colt with her. Loose them and bring them to me. If any one say aught to you, ye shall say: "The Lord hath need of them," and straightway he will send them.'

They went, and found the ass and the colt, not in a man's stable, or courtyard, but, as Peter says—at the gate without in the open street. They began to untie them.

'What are you doing there, loosing the ass and the colt?' asked the owner.

They gave the password that Jesus had arranged with the man—'The Master hath need of them'—and at once he let them take the animals. So they hurried back to Jesus, and threw their own cloaks on the ass. He got

[1] Zechariah ix. 9.

A donkey and colt by Bethphage on the Mount of Olives

astride and began to move towards Jerusalem, which was still hidden on the other side of the ridge of the Mount of Olives. The simple act set the glowing enthusiasm of the multitude ablaze. In all their differing ideas of what the Messiah would be and do, they all remembered the words of Zechariah:

> 'Behold thy King cometh unto thee,
> Meek, and riding upon an ass.'

'The Son of David', as blind Bar-Timaeus had called him, was riding into David's city upon an ass. They broke out into cries: 'Save us. Hosanna!'

From the palm-trees bright with the spring growth they tore leafy branches and strewed them on the winding way. To show their adoration of their King, they even cast down their cloaks so that the donkey might walk over them. Moving across the saddle of the mountain and round a sweeping curve on its western side, they could see across the Kidron Ravine to the corner of the City of David on which the Temple shone. At that point where the descent of the Mount of Olives began, the whole multitude broke into exultant rejoicing, singing to the praise of God for all the mighty works that they had seen Jesus do, chanting: 'Blessed is he that cometh in the name of the Lord.'

The sound carried across the valley. The people came pouring out. Pharisees in the crowd were disturbed and angry.

'See', they said one to another, 'we make no headway. The whole world has run after him.'

Elbowing their way through the mass of people to the side of Jesus, they said: 'Master, rebuke your disciples.'

'I tell you,' he replied, 'if these shall hold their peace, the very stones will cry out.'

Within him, even as he spoke, the deep well-springs of pent-up feeling broke. Tears came to his eyes; he wept as he looked at the lovely city, called by David, 'The City of

Peace—Jerusalem', which was, indeed, the very soul of his nation. He loved it as the City of God. Jerusalem had, through its leaders in the Temple, again and again rejected him and was even at that moment plotting his death. They waited for a Messiah coming in glorious battle-array to sweep away the Romans and set up a Jewish throne in the City. That way—Jesus saw—lay frightful ruin; streets running with blood as Rome took—as she always did take —terrible vengeance on those who rebelled against her rule.

The whole city was stirred; 'shaken as by an earthquake,' says Matthew.

'Who is this?' demanded the citizens as they poured out to meet the oncoming multitude.

'This is the prophet, Jesus, from Nazareth, of Galilee,' was the reply.

So Jesus rode up the street into Jerusalem. Alighting, he went into the Temple. Orders had been given for his arrest. But it was too dangerous to carry them out. Annas and Caiaphas and the Sanhedrin could see that to attempt his arrest among the thousands of pilgrims, who believed that he was the Messiah, would cause such a rebellion as might shatter their power, and so they held their hand, but only set to work with subtle cunning to discover some weak place in his defences, some traitor even amongst his own followers.

Their chance would come when the pilgrims were asleep. But in this Jesus baffled them. Before nightfall he turned, and with the Twelve went out of the city across the ravine and over the ridge of the Mount of Olives, back to the safe retreat of Bethany and the loving fellowship of Lazarus, Martha, and Mary.

CHAPTER XV

TRAPS AND A PLOT

ALREADY Jesus had decided to attack the power of Annas and Caiaphas where it was strongest—in their command of money. At dawn he started back to the city and went to the Temple.

Isaiah had said: 'Mine house shall be called "A House of Prayer for all Peoples".'[1] But what was the reality to which Annas and his family had degraded it? The only true description was in Jeremiah's stinging phrase—'A Den of Robbers'.[2]

As Jesus entered the great outer court of the Temple, the lowing of calves, the bleating of sheep, the murmur of doves filled his ears. The merchants, who paid vast sums of money to Annas and his family on their sales, were charging outrageous prices for these animals to pilgrims who came to sacrifice. A man would have to pay, for instance, as much as a golden denar—some fifteen shillings —for a pair of doves worth a few pence; because they had been passed by the Temple authorities as free from blemish.

How was this peasant from Tyre, that merchant from Alexandria, yonder scholar from Athens, or this metal-worker from Damascus to pay for his lamb or dove? Each of them had come with the money of his country. But they could only buy in the Temple with the shekels of the Temple which had no 'graven image' on them. So hundreds of money-changers sat at little tables and changed silver Greek drachmae or Roman denarii into the half-shekel that every grown man pilgrim must pay into the Temple treasure. This was the fourth day before the feast, and the majority of the pilgrims who had already arrived were from foreign lands. The money-changers made large

[1] Isaiah lvi. 7.   [2] Jeremiah vii. 11.

profits. In changing the pilgrims' money they cheated them. Was it not the exact truth that God's 'House of Prayer for all Peoples', was a robbers' den?

Jesus' face grew stern. His eyes flashed. Compassion for the robbed pilgrims, indignation against these false shepherds who fleeced them, zeal for the pure worship of the Holy Loving God filled his soul.

'It is written,' he cried aloud, above the hubbub, ' "My house shall be called a house of prayer for all peoples". But ye make it "a den of robbers".'

He began to drive them out. One money-changer's table and then another went spinning; the silver and bronze coins went clinking across the stone floor. Panic began as the pilgrims, full of wrath against the men who had stripped them of their money, stood menacing, as the dove-sellers and the money-changers fled.

Annas and Caiaphas were furious, but could do nothing at that instant. They would have given anything to crush him there and then. But one look at the pilgrims showed the high priest and his hangers-on that they would be torn limb from limb if they laid a hand on him. The very boys began to cheer.

'Hosanna,' they cried, 'to the Son of David.'

Pharisees, horrified at this, asked Jesus angrily: 'Hearest thou what these are saying?'

He answered their question with another: 'Did ye never read: "Out of the mouth of babes and sucklings thou hast perfected praise"?'

Sick men, with others lame and blind, hobbled or were led or carried to him; and he healed them. The evening came on. Again he went, as he did on all the first four evenings of that week, to pray and to sleep on the Mount of Olives, either in Bethany or wrapped in his cloak under the olives. For the Temple police might have tracked him down if he had spent the nights in Jerusalem; and when the pilgrims had gone to sleep, might have arrested him under cover of the darkness. In the day-time they were helpless, for, as Luke said: 'They could not find what they might do; for all the people hung upon him, listening.'

If he could not arrest Jesus, however, Caiaphas was not idle. He and his men, with the help of Annas, worked on two schemes. One was to make a series of traps. They planned questions which they were sure would trap him into saying things that would make him guilty both of blasphemy and of rebellion against Rome. Then they could call in Pilate, who had, as usual, come up from Caesarea to Jerusalem at the feast-time in case of emergency, and he would condemn him.

The second scheme was to get one of Jesus' followers to lead them to a place where they could arrest him when the pilgrims were not about.

The traps were very crafty. Jesus came up from the Mount with the Twelve in the morning and was at once greeted by a deputation from Caiaphas and the Sanhedrin. They went straight to the point. Referring to his sensational act of cleansing the Temple, they asked a simple, natural question: 'Tell us: by what authority doest thou these things? Or who is he that gave thee this authority?'

They were sure he would walk into this trap. Caiaphas and the Sanhedrin were the constituted authorities in the Temple under the Roman rule. If Jesus set himself above them, and Pilate, then he was a rebel; if he was not above them, he had no authority! The crowd of pilgrims listened intently.

'*I* also will ask you a question,' replied Jesus, surely with a smile; 'and tell me: The baptism of John, was it from heaven or from men?'

Their faces fell; they fingered their beards; they whispered to one another.

'If we shall say, "From heaven," said one, 'he will say, "Why did ye not believe him?"'

'Yes,' another whispered back, 'but if we say, "From men," all these pilgrims will stone us, for they are sure that he is a prophet.'

At last, in utter bewilderment, they stuttered: 'We know not.'

'Neither tell I you by what authority I do these things,' replied Jesus.

Great was the joy of the pilgrims at seeing this trap fail.

Jesus now turned the tables on them by another question arising out of a tiny parable.

'What think ye of this,' he asked, 'A certain man had two sons. To the elder he said: "Son, go work in my vineyard to-day." And he replied, "I go, Sir," but went not. To the younger he gave the same command. "I go not," he replied, but went. Which of the two,' Jesus asked, 'did the will of his father?'

'The second,' they answered.

'I tell you that even the publicans and the harlots go into the Kingdom of God before you.'

Jesus was thinking of Matthew, Zacchaeus, and Mary of Magdala.

'Hear another parable,' he said, speaking not to the deputation that was seated around him, but to the crowd beyond.

'A man planted a vineyard, and set a hedge about it, and digged a pit for the winepress, and built a tower, and let it out to husbandmen, and went into another country. And at the season he sent to the husbandmen a servant, that he might receive from the husbandmen of the fruits of the vineyard. And they took him and beat him and sent him away empty. And again he sent unto them another servant; and him they wounded in the head, and handled shamefully. And he sent another; and him they killed: and many others; beating some, and killing some. He had yet one, a beloved son: he sent him last unto them, saying, "They will reverence my son." But those husbandmen said among themselves, "This is the heir; come and let us kill him, and the inheritance shall be ours." And they took him, and killed him, and cast him forth out of the vineyard. What therefore will the lord of the vineyard do? He will come and destroy the husbandmen, and will give the vineyard unto others. Have ye not read even this scripture; "The stone which the builders rejected, the same was made the head of the corner: this was from the Lord, and it is marvellous in our eyes"?' [1]

This direct attack was too much for the Sanhedrin. They were as amazed at the superb mastery by which he had quietly broken their trap as they were furious at having made themselves ridiculous. They rose and left him.

A still more artful trap was set for him by a group of Pharisees. They sent some young disciples to ask a question that seemed bound to make him either side with Rome (which would turn the pilgrims against him) or with the patriots, which would make him a rebel against Rome.

'Master,' said the new group, trying to blind him by flattery, 'we know that thou art true and carest not for any one: for thou regardest not the person of men but of a truth teachest the way of God. Is it right to pay tribute to Caesar or not? Shall we give or shall we not give?'

If Jesus said 'Yes', he would seem to be no patriot: if he said 'No' he would be a rebel.

'Why tempt me?' said Jesus. 'Show me a silver penny.'

One of them pulled one out of his pocket.

'Whose is this image and this superscription?' Jesus asked, with his finger on the face of the Emperor.

'Caesar's,' they answered.

'Render unto Caesar the things that are Caesar's,' he replied, 'and to God the things that are God's.'

That trap also failed.

Jesus had never said that Caesar's rule was entirely good. But he had shown the justice of recognizing by the tribute that Caesar brought them good roads, protection

[1] Mark xii. 1-11.

from raiding Arabs and robbers on land, and from pirates by sea. These gifts of strong government deserved recognition. They made Jerusalem and Judaea rich, for only so could the pilgrims come and commerce grow.

This second deputation walked away in gloomy silence, crestfallen. For they, too, had failed as ridiculously as the first group.

Jesus went on to attack the Scribes and the Pharisees, the whole ruling caste that treated the Law and the Temple as their own preserve and gloried in the outward show of goodness.

'Beware of the scribes, which desire to walk in long robes, and to have salutations in the market-places and chief seats in the synagogues, and chief places at feasts: they which devour widows' houses, and for a pretence make long prayers; these shall receive greater condemnation.'

Weary of these arguments with men whose hard hearts and clever brains were bent on his destruction, Jesus walked from the Terrace, where he had been talking, to the Treasury, where a constant stream of pilgrims went by as they paid their half-shekel of Temple tribute. The Treasury was in the Court of Women, which, it will be remembered, was so called because, although all Jews, men and women, could enter it, no woman was allowed to go farther in, that is, into the Place of Sacrifice.

By the wall of the Treasury were thirteen strange-looking objects, like large trumpets standing on the large end. They were really great money-boxes. The pilgrims put the gifts in at the small end at the top. The first two were for the half-shekel gift; the third was for thanksgiving, for instance, by a mother when her boy or girl recovered from an illness. Jesus sat close by looking at the men and women as they passed by. Near him stood Peter and the other disciples. Here came a wealthy merchant in a silk cloak who drew from his pouch a handful of silver and dropped it in. There followed a Scribe who made sure that every one should see him drop in his gift. A poor widow came along in dark, worn clothes that she had darned many times. In her hand she held tight two tiny copper coins. These lepta or mites, which did not amount to one half-penny, she had saved with difficulty, for she was very poor.

'See,' said Jesus to Peter, at his elbow, 'of a truth I say unto you, this poor widow cast in more than they all: for all these did of their plenty cast in to the treasury; but she of her want did cast in all the living that she had.'

So the woman moved on and was lost in the crowd, little guessing that among all the ugly deeds done, the cruel words spoken, and vile plots hatched in the Temple on that day, her little act would shine, a lovely jewel, as long as human speech lasts on the earth.

Near to Jesus, among those watching, were some men from a far-away land. Indeed, they were not Jews by blood. They were called Greeks. These men, however, had been converted from the worship of pagan gods like Zeus or Apollo to the Jewish worship of the one invisible God. So they had sailed from their land to Judaea for the Passover. They had watched Jesus' entry into Jerusalem, seen him cleanse the Temple, wondered at his powers of healing, listened to his teaching. They desired greatly to talk with him and learn more from him. But they were too shy to go straight to him.

One of the disciples had a Greek name meaning 'lover of horses', Philip. So it may be that one of his parents was of Greek origin. In any case, the Greeks found him easy to approach.

'We would see Jesus,' they said to him.

Philip himself was rather timid, so he consulted the other disciple with a Greek name—Andrew, 'the Manly'. Together they went to Jesus.

'Here are Greeks who would see you,' said Andrew.

'The time has come,' Jesus exclaimed, 'for the Son of Man to be glorified.'

What he saw at that moment came true in a few years. Men speaking the language of those 'Greeks' went out across the world of the Roman Empire, sowing the seed among every people on earth.

Then he spoke to those Greeks and to all around words that tell by what sacrifice alone the Kingdom of God can spread in the world.

'Verily, verily, I say unto you, except a grain of wheat fall into the earth and die, it abideth by itself alone; but if it die, it beareth much fruit. He that loveth his life, loseth it; and he that hateth his life in this world shall keep it unto life eternal. If any man serve me, let him follow me; and where I am, there shall also my servant be: if any man serve me, him will my Father honour.'

Swiftly his mind turned from the glory of the open door into the great world to the narrow, dreadful gate of death through which he must go: 'Except a grain of wheat fall into the earth and *die*.'

The anguish of it tore from him words charged with suffering. 'Now is my soul troubled; and what shall I say? "Father, save me from this hour?" But for this cause came I unto this hour.'

Then, knowing what torture it was going to cost him, Jesus made the decision. He cried aloud: 'Father, glorify thy name.'

A deep Voice spoke. Some said it thundered. Others said, 'No, an angel hath spoken to him.'

The Voice said to Jesus: 'I have glorified it and will glorify it again.'

Jesus saw the crisis of the hour and the victory ahead: 'Now is the judgement of this world. Now shall the prince of this world be cast out. And I, if I be lifted up from the earth, will draw all men unto myself.'

With this Jesus turned his back on the Temple courts

and went out, never to enter its gates again. With his men
he crossed to the Mount of Olives. There, in the spring
sunshine, he talked with them. He told them the last
stories they were to hear from his lips to illustrate what the
Kingdom of Heaven is like. He told a tale of bridesmaids
at a village wedding such as all of the Twelve had shared
in. The wedding takes place at the bridegroom's house;
but he keeps out of the way all day while the feast is being
prepared, and in the evening comes down the village
street with young men companions carrying torches and
the bridesmaids go out from the house with lighted lamps
to meet them.

'Then shall the kingdom of heaven be likened unto ten virgins,
which took their lamps, and went forth to meet the bridegroom.
And five of them were foolish, and five were wise. For the foolish,
when they took their lamps, took no oil with them, but the wise took
oil in their vessels with their lamps. Now while the bridegroom
tarried, they all slumbered and slept. But at midnight there is a cry,
"Behold, the bridegroom! Come ye forth to meet him." Then all those
virgins arose, and trimmed their lamps. And the foolish said unto the
wise, "Give us of your oil; for our lamps are going out." But the
wise answered, saying, "Peradventure there will not be enough for us
and you: go ye rather to them that sell, and buy for yourselves." And
while they went away to buy, the bridegroom came; and they that
were ready went in with him to the marriage feast: and the door was
shut. Afterward come also the other virgins, saying, "Lord, Lord,
open to us." But he answered and said, "Verily, I say unto you, I know
you not." Watch therefore, for ye know not the day nor the hour.'

He then told a very different story about a travelling
merchant similar in some ways to the story that he told
at Jericho, but, as we shall see, absolutely different in
meaning.

'It is as when a man, going into another country, called his own
servants, and delivered unto them his goods. And unto one he gave
five talents, to another two, to another one; to each according to his
several ability; and he went on his journey. Straightway he that
received the five talents went and traded with them, and made other
five talents. In like manner he also that received the two gained

other two. But he that received the one went away and digged in the earth, and hid his lord's money. After a long time the lord of those servants cometh, and maketh a reckoning with them. And he that received the five talents came and brought other five talents, saying, "Lord, thou deliveredst unto me five talents: lo, I have gained other five talents." His lord said unto him, "Well done, good and faithful servant: thou hast been faithful over a few things, I will set thee over many things: enter thou into the joy of thy lord." And he also that received the two talents came and said, "Lord, thou deliveredst unto me two talents: lo, I have gained other two talents." His lord said unto him. "Well done, good and faithful servant; thou hast been faithful over a few things, I will set thee over many things: enter thou into the joy of thy lord." And he also that had received the one talent came and said, "Lord, I knew thee that thou art a hard man, reaping where thou didst not sow, and gathering where thou didst not scatter: and I was afraid, and went away and hid thy talent in the earth: lo, thou hast thine own." But his lord answered and said unto him, "Thou wicked and slothful servant, thou knewest that I reap where I sowed not, and gather where I did not scatter; thou oughtest therefore to have put my money to the bankers, and at my coming I should have received back mine own with interest. Take ye away therefore the talent from him, and give it unto him that hath the ten talents. For unto every one that hath shall be given, and he shall have abundance: but from him that hath not, even that which he hath shall be taken away. And cast ye out the unprofitable servant into outer darkness: there shall be the weeping and gnashing of teeth." '

These servants were trusted with very large amounts. For each Greek talent was worth about £240. The disciples, as they listened, would recall the Parable of the Pounds that Jesus told at Jericho. It will help us to see the different meaning of each if we put the points down side by side:

Parable of the Pounds.	*Parable of the Talents.*
A prince who does not know the differing ability and character of his servants.	A merchant who knows the different ability and character of his servants.
His aim is to find out their ability so that he can tell which of his servants should be trusted to govern large or small groups of cities in his land.	His aim is to get profit by the trading skill of his servants.

Therefore

The prince gives all the servants exactly the same small amount so that he can judge from the difference in the results the differing capacities of the servants.

The good servants get differing rewards according to their differing success in using the same amount of money. That is to say, the reward is for skill loyally used.

The reward of greater skill wedded to zeal for the master is greater responsibility: 'Have authority over ten cities.'

The punishment of not using the gift is death. This is an actual fact of natural law. Any muscle, for instance, that is never used, atrophies.

The merchant gives large and different sums, sharply graded according to the servants' abilities. He expects to get the biggest profit from the cleverest, but some profit from all.

The two good servants get exactly the same reward, although their success is different, because they have both done their best with what talents they have, even although the talents given to them differ. That is to say, the reward is for faithful zeal.

The reward of loving work for the master, whether the skill is small or great, is to enjoy personal friendship with him: 'Share your master's board.'

The punishment of not giving loyal service to the master is exile from his friendship and company.

As the day drew towards its close the shepherds led their flocks of sheep and herds of goats along the hill-side towards the folds, as they do now every day in that same valley. The lambs and kids were all mixed together, as were their mothers, the sheep and the goats. Coming to the two folds, one for sheep, one for goats, the shepherd stood and divided them, sending the goats to the left and the sheep to the right.

The disciples watched this, as they gazed, too, upon the thousands of pilgrims going into Jerusalem, and the sinking sun seemed to set the golden roof of the Temple ablaze. In contrast, far away to the left, rose the smoke of the fire that consumed the refuse of Jerusalem, an everlasting fire, for it was made up every day by loads of filth and rubbish from the city. This fire was called the fire of Ge-Henna, i.e. of the Valley of Hinnom in which it burned.

Out of those things—the sheep and goats, the crowd, the shining gold, and the fire—Jesus made his parable.

'But when the Son of man shall come in his glory, and all the angels with him, then shall he sit on the throne of his glory: and before him shall be gathered all the nations: and he shall separate them one from another, as the shepherd separateth the sheep from the goats: and he shall set the sheep on his right hand, but the goats on the left. Then shall the King say unto them on his right hand, "Come, ye blessed of my Father, inherit the kingdom prepared for you from the foundation of the world: for I was an hungred, and ye gave me meat: I was thirsty, and ye gave me drink: I was a stranger, and ye took me in; naked, and ye clothed me: I was sick, and ye visited me: I was in prison, and ye came unto me." Then shall the righteous answer him, saying, "Lord, when saw we thee an hungred, and fed thee? or athirst, and gave thee drink? And when saw we thee a stranger, and took thee in? or naked, and clothed thee? And when saw we thee sick, or in prison, and came unto thee?" And the King shall answer and say unto them, "Verily, I say unto you, inasmuch as ye did it unto one of these my brethren, even these least, ye did it unto me." Then shall he say also unto them on the left hand, "Depart from me, ye cursed, into the eternal fire which is prepared for the devil and his angels: for I was an hungred, and ye gave me no meat: I was thirsty, and ye gave me no drink: I was a stranger, and ye took me not in; naked, and ye clothed me not; sick, and in prison, and ye visited me not." Then shall they also answer, saying, "Lord, when saw we thee an hungred, or athirst, or a stranger, or naked, or sick, or in prison, and did not minister unto thee?" Then shall he answer them, saying, "Verily, I say unto you, inasmuch as ye did it not unto one of these least, ye did it not unto me." '

So the sun set and they slept. But not all—Judas of Kerioth, the only southerner among the Twelve, went off alone on a secret errand. He recrossed the Kidron, and climbed the hill on the south-east of the Temple till he reached the gates of Caiaphas' palace. Then he was led into the hall where Annas and Caiaphas sat with others of the Sanhedrin.

'I am a disciple of this Jesus, whom you seek to take. I can help you.'

They were very glad at this opportunity. It would now be possible to have Jesus put to death before the Passover: for they feared that the great day of the feast might work the pilgrims into such a frenzy of enthusiasm that they would rise against both the Sanhedrin and against Rome, and try to make him King. Rome would come down with her merciless hand and wipe out all the power of the Chief Priests and take sole despotic control. It was better, as Caiaphas had said, that one man should perish rather than the nation.

They offered Judas a miserable bribe: it was the amount paid under Moses' law as blood-money for having killed a slave! But, as a matter of fact, money was not Judas' real aim, fond though he was of it.

Why, then, should one chosen by Jesus, who had been with him for many months, and had gone out to preach the Good News of the Kingdom—why should he be ready to sell his master for less than the value of five pounds? Caiaphas could have been persuaded easily to pay twenty times that amount.

Judas was ambitious. He had seen himself (being treasurer of the common purse of the Twelve) as one day to be the Lord High Treasurer in the Kingdom when Jesus was on the throne; just as James and John had asked to be Chief Viziers. Only four days ago he had believed that his ambition was on the point of being realized, when Jesus rode into the city hailed by crowds as the Son of David. Now, to Judas' keen disappointment, Jesus was going straight towards execution as a criminal, through his refusal to head a rebellion by using the miraculous powers that God had given him. Judas decided to force Jesus' hand. He would lead Caiaphas' forces to arrest Jesus. Then one of two things must happen. Either Jesus would call to his aid an army of the angels of God, as Judas was sure he could, and win the throne; or Jesus would be executed and thus the miserable farce would be over.

Judas was in agonies of jealousy, too. Over and over again, at special crises, as for instance, at the Mount of Transfiguration, or at the raising of Jairus' daughter, Jesus always chose Simon Peter and John and James to go with him—never Judas. The very fact of his love for Jesus made his jealousy the wilder and madder. Jealousy, passion for power, foiled ambition, wounded pride, and a desperate chance of forcing Jesus' hand—these led Judas to betray the Master he loved

What could Judas betray? No one in Jerusalem except the Twelve had ever heard Jesus say the words that would make him a rebel in the eyes of the Law, that is, that he was Messiah. Judas could tell Caiaphas that. This would make Caiaphas decide on putting that question straight to Jesus, which—as we shall see—he did.

What Caiaphas most of all needed, however, was what Luke tells us Judas now plotted for, the opportunity to deliver Jesus up 'in the absence of the multitude'.

Meanwhile Jesus, desiring greatly that he should take his Passover supper with the Twelve in Jerusalem, also made secret plans to that end. They were bound to be secret plans, for if it were known where he was supping, Caiaphas would send and arrest him in the night. In Jerusalem was a woman disciple of Jesus named Mary, whose husband owned a large house with a room big enough for him to give supper to the Twelve. The people of the house were loyal friends. Jesus asked them to let him use their large upper room for the supper. He could not even tell the disciples where the supper was to be, for he had read what lay in Judas' heart. So a wonderfully simple but clever signal was arranged. One of Mary's men-slaves should carry a water-jar and wait by one of the city gates. In Palestine a man, if no woman is at hand to help him, may carry a water-jar, for he must have water from the spring or the reservoir; but it is very rarely that he does so.

The following day Jesus sent Peter and John into Jerusalem to prepare the Passover.

'Where wilt thou that we go and make ready for thee to eat the Passover?' they asked.

'Go into the city,' he replied, 'and there you shall meet a man bearing a pitcher of water: follow him; and wheresoever he shall enter in, say to the good man of the house, "The Master saith, 'Where is my guest-chamber, where I shall eat the Passover with my disciples?'" And he will himself show you a large upper room furnished and ready: and there make ready for us.'

So they set off on their errand, not knowing any more than did Judas, who was carefully listening, where the supper was to be. Why, however, was Jesus taking the Passover supper twenty-four hours too soon? For it was not due until the eve of the Sabbath. Jesus knew that Annas and Caiaphas were set on his death before the feast; yet he was anxious to join his disciples in one last Passover feast which they could celebrate year by year in remembrance of him. He, therefore, celebrated the Passover a whole day earlier, as was permitted when the true Passover was on the Sabbath. This was permitted in order to avoid the danger of breaking the Law of the Sabbath by working at the preparation and service of that meal on that day.

As Peter and John came to the city gate they saw the man with the water-jar. He led them along winding streets on the south side of the city to a house where they were admitted by a slave-girl. The master of the house came out and they spoke the words that Jesus had given them. He led them up twenty-one stone steps to a balcony that had a door into a large upper room. Couches on which to recline at dinner were arranged in horseshoe formation. The copper-basin, water-jar, and towel with which a slave (or at times the youngest person present) always washed the dust of the streets from the feet of the guests were ready. On the low table between the couches stood the two-handled chalice for the Passover wine.

The food was then prepared; the paste of fruits and nuts made into a thin brick to bring to mind the slavery of the Israelites in Egypt; the thin, flat loaves of bread into which the woman had put no yeast, to bring to remembrance the bread that those Israelites had made in haste when starting to flee from the land of Pharaoh; the sacrificial lamb free from spot.

Jesus stood on the Mount for the last time. He was still free. He could, if he would, leave Jerusalem, go the way of Bethany to beloved friends, or back to the sunny hills round Nazareth and the blue waters of the shining Lake. Or he could take that steep, hard path to Jerusalem, which would bring him to his death on the cross. Because he loved his Father, God, and all men whom God has made, he took that path of shame, when he might have revelled in the loveliness of flower and sky and sea, of the song of birds, of the prattle of children, and of the brave companionship of his friends.

Greater love hath no man than this—nor greater courage

CHAPTER XVI

BETRAYAL

THE Passover moon shone down into the narrow streets as Jesus led his men to the house with the upper room. Entering the courtyard they were led up the steps outside the house. The host opened the door and welcomed them in; then he left the Twelve with Jesus there.

Taking off their sandals the disciples began to take their places. No slave was present to wash their feet. Who would do that for them? Not one of them was ready to lower himself to this task. To make matters worse, the Twelve actually began to wrangle as to who should take the higher places at the table.

Jesus rose, threw off his outer garment, twisted a towel about his waist, took up the water-jar, filled the copper basin, and began to do the work of the slave, washing the feet of his guests. Repentance burned in the hearts of the Twelve for their hateful pride and quarrelsome ambitions. Impulsive, hot-blooded Peter could not bear it. As Jesus knelt at his feet, he cried: 'Lord, dost thou wash my feet?'

'What I do thou knowest not now,' said Jesus gently, 'but thou shalt understand later.'

'Thou shalt never wash my feet,' Peter exclaimed.

'Thou hast no part with me, if I wash thee not,' Jesus replied.

The impulsive fellow leapt to the other extreme.

'Lord, not my feet only, but also my hands and my head.'

'He that is bathed,' Jesus said, 'needeth not save to wash his feet; he is clean all over. And you are clean,' he continued, and then he exclaimed, 'but not all.'

Having gone round all his shamefaced disciples, he took his garments and sat down again.

'Know ye what I have done to you?' he asked. 'Ye call me

"Master", and "Lord", and ye say well; for so I am. If I then, the Lord and the Master, have washed your feet, ye also ought to wash one another's feet. For I have given you an example, that ye also should do as I have done to you. Verily, verily, I say unto you, A servant is not greater than his lord; neither one that is sent greater than he that sent him. If ye know these things, blessed are ye if ye do them.

Then he told them of the great longing with which he had looked forward to this supper with them. So the meal went on according to the order of the Passover supper, with the passing of the chalice containing the juice of the vine, then the bitter paste, and the lamb. Taking bread in his hands Jesus gave thanks to God for it and, as is the custom at the Passover, broke it in pieces. To each of the Twelve he gave a piece, saying, as he did so: 'Take, eat; this is my body which is given for you: this do in remembrance of me.'

Then he took the cup of red wine mingled with water and said: 'This cup is the new covenant in my blood: this do, as oft as ye drink it, in remembrance of me.'

At his side he saw on the table the clutching, nervous fingers of Judas.

'Behold,' said Jesus, 'the hand of him that betrays me is with me on the table.'

His men were horror-struck.

'In very truth,' he repeated, 'one of you shall betray me.'

'Is it I, Master?' one after another they asked, trembling.

Judas, the traitor, dared not keep silence: in deadly fear he said: 'Surely it is not I?'

'Is it not?' said Jesus quietly, in a low voice that only carried to Judas on Jesus' left, and escaped Peter who was beyond John on Jesus' right.

Peter leaned over to John who was resting on Jesus' shoulder and asked: 'Tell us who it is that he means.'

John, leaning back on Jesus, whispered: 'Master, who is it?'

Jesus, speaking quietly, said: 'He that dippeth with me in the dish, the same shall betray me.'

Breaking a piece of bread, he bent it to make a spoon, dipped it in the dish and handed it to Judas. Then he said: 'What thou must do, do quickly.'

Judas rose, strapped on his sandals, swung his cloak over his shoulders, and threw open the door. John, who alone shared the tragic knowledge, followed every movement. He never forgot that oblong of dark starry sky seen in the few seconds while Judas plunged through the open doorway. 'It was,' he tells us, 'night.'

They sang the 118th Psalm, as always at the Passover supper:

> 'The Lord is on my side;
> I will not fear:
> What men can do unto me.
>
> .   .   .   .   .   .
>
> The stone which the builders rejected
> Is become the head of the corner.
> This is the Lord's doing;
> It is marvellous in our eyes.'

Then Jesus spoke to the group of faithful disciples:

'I am the true vine, and my Father is the husbandman. Every branch in me that beareth not fruit, he taketh it away: and every branch that beareth fruit, he cleanseth it, that it may bear more fruit. Already ye are clean because of the word which I have spoken unto you. Abide in me, and I in you. As the branch cannot bear fruit of itself, except it abide in the vine: so neither can ye, except ye abide in me. I am the vine, ye are the branches: he that abideth in me, and I in him, the same beareth much fruit: for apart from me ye can do nothing. If a man abide not in me, he is cast forth as a branch, and is withered; and they gather them, and cast them into the fire, and they are burned. If ye abide in me, and my words abide in you, ask whatsoever ye will, and it shall be done unto you. Herein is my Father glorified, that ye bear much fruit; and so shall ye be my disciples. Even as the Father hath loved me, I also have loved you: abide ye in my love. If ye keep my commandments, ye shall abide in my love; even as I have kept my Father's commandments, and abide in his love.

'These things have I spoken unto you, that my joy may be in you, and that your joy may be fulfilled. This is my commandment, that ye love one another, even as I have loved you. Greater love hath no man than this, that a man lay down his life for his friends. Ye are my friends, if ye do the things which I command you. No longer do I call you servants; for the servant knoweth not what his lord doeth: but I have called you friends; for all things that I heard from my Father I have made known unto you. Ye did not choose me, but I chose you, and appointed you, that ye should go and bear fruit, and that your fruit should abide: that whatsoever ye shall ask of the Father in my name, he may give it you. These things I command you, that ye may love one another.'

He went on to tell them how he was leaving them and how they were to face the days when men would want to kill them too.

'I give you a new commandment,' Jesus repeated, ' "Love one another—as I have loved you." By this shall all men know that ye are my disciples, if ye have love to one another.'

Peter's love for his Master could not bear the thought of separation.

'Lord, whither goest thou?' he asked.

'Whither I go, thou canst not follow now,' Jesus replied.

'Lord, why cannot I follow thee even now? I will lay down my life for thee,' he cried, his whole soul in his impulsive face.

'Lay down thy life for me? Wilt thou?' Jesus asked, looking into the very soul of the Peter whom he knew better than Simon knew himself. 'Verily, verily, I say unto thee, the cock shall not crow till thou hast denied me thrice.'

Peter's eyes were filled with pain.

'Let not your heart be troubled,' said Jesus. 'Ye believe in God, believe also in me. In my Father's house are many mansions; if it were not so, I would have told you; for I go to prepare a place for you. And if I go and prepare a place for you, I come again, and will receive you unto myself; that where I am, there ye may be also. And whither I go, ye know the way.'

'Lord,' objected Thomas, from across the table, 'we know not whither thou goest, how can we know the way?'

Jesus replied:

'I am the way, and the truth and the life: no one cometh unto the Father but by me. If ye had known me, ye would have known my Father also; from henceforth ye know him, and have seen him.'

'Lord,' interrupted Philip, 'shew us the Father, that will satisfy us.'

'Have I been,' said Jesus, 'so long time with you, and dost thou not know me, Philip? he that hath seen me hath seen the Father; how sayest thou, "Shew us the Father?" Believest thou not that I am in the Father, and the Father in me? . . . Verily, verily, I say unto you, He that believeth on me, the works that I do shall he do also; and greater works than these shall he do; because I go unto the Father. And whatsoever ye shall ask in my name, that will I do, that the Father may be glorified in the Son. If ye shall ask me anything in my name, that will I do.'

He spoke more words to them, and then, standing, said: 'Arise, let us go hence.'

As they stood on the balcony of the courtyard, in the night air, Jesus lifted his face to heaven and prayed for his men whom he loved so deeply and was now leaving defenceless.

'Holy Father, keep them in thy name, whom thou hast given to me, that they may be one, even as we are.'

'Neither for these only do I pray,' he cried, his thought going out to the wider world of those who did and would in days to come believe on him, 'but for them also that believe on me through their word; that they may all be one; even as thou, Father, art in me and I in thee, that they also may be in us: that the world may believe that thou didst send me.'

So they went together down the steps and out from the city gates down to the Kidron Valley, while behind them young John Mark, pulled by the strange power of this man, came, wrapped round him a sheet he had snatched up as he awoke at the sound of the Master's voice in prayer on the courtyard steps of his father's house.

It was midnight, the hour when the angel 'passed over' the homes of the Israelites in Egypt.

Meanwhile Judas had walked rapidly to Caiaphas' palace below the south wall of the Temple. He was expected. A group of the Temple police were waiting. A company of Roman soldiers had been ordered from the Antonia garrison, for they alone could make an arrest outside the Temple area. Torches were lighted. Judas called to the captain to follow him. Judas knew that Jesus would go to the accustomed place on the lower slope of the Mount of Olives, near the Kidron gully.

'Whomsoever I shall kiss,' said Judas, 'that is he; take him and lead him away safely.'

So with lantern and torch they stumbled down the Roman street into the valley, and crossing the Kidron by Absalom's Tomb, moved diagonally up the lower slope of the Mount of Olives towards the Garden of the Oil Press— Gethsemane.

From the shadow of the olive-trees a man suddenly stepped out into the moonlight to greet them. He had nothing in his hands: they were armed with staves and swords and javelins: but they fell back.

Jesus and the Eleven had already come down the hill. As they neared Gethsemane, he suddenly distressed them terribly by saying: 'You will all be made to stumble because of me to-night. As the Scripture says: "I will smite the shepherd and the sheep shall be scattered." '

Peter, ever explosive, exclaimed: 'Even if I must die with thee, I will not deny thee.'

They all said the same. By this time they were at their familiar resting-place in the garden with its grey boulders, its olive-trees, and the stone press for crushing the oil from the olives.

'Sit here,' said he to his men, 'while I pray.'

He took with him, however, the three whom he always took in the hours of crisis and strain, Peter, James, and John. And at that hour his heart was wrung as it never had been in his life.

'My soul is exceeding sorrowful,' he said. 'Yes, even unto death: abide ye here and watch.'

Going a stone's throw from them he threw himself on the ground. 'Abba,' he cried, using the word of a child calling to his Father, 'O my Father, if it be possible let this cup pass away from me; nevertheless, not what I will, but what thou wilt.'

He rose and walked back to his three friends. They were fast asleep. With the very threat of death hovering over their Master, with agony of spirit tearing him, these men who a few minutes earlier had sworn to die rather than forsake him, slept. Only John Mark, hidden in the trees, witnessed and heard the agony of the Master and told later to the world in his Gospel, that dread struggle on the issue of which the destiny of mankind hung.

'Simon,' said Jesus, 'sleepest thou? Couldst thou not watch one hour? Watch,' he added, 'and pray that you enter not into temptation. The spirit indeed is willing,' said he of himself, 'but the flesh is weak.'

Again he went away a stone's throw and cried to the Father.

'O my Father, if this cannot pass away except I drink it, thy will be done.'

Returning once more to his disciples he found them heavy with sleep, and grievously ashamed when his touch awakened them. 'Our eyes were very heavy', Peter told John Mark later, 'and we knew not what to answer him.' So Jesus a third time wrestled in spirit. He had walked steadily towards this hour of death for months. It was not his courage that failed now. What broke Jesus' heart was the awful tragedy of his nation. Its blind leaders were rejecting the love of God that Jesus showed in his life, and were dragging their nation to destruction.

Now Jesus saw through the trees the moving torches and heard the clank of steel as the soldiers and the mob of Temple officers came near. He went to the three.

'Still asleep,' he exclaimed sadly. 'Still taking your ease. Enough! The hour is come. The Son of Man is betrayed into the hands of wicked men. Arise, let us be going. Behold, he that betrayeth me is at hand.'

The three were indeed awake now; they joined the others. The mob came on. Suddenly Jesus stepped forward into the moonlight. There, in the dead of night, with the glory of God in his face after the agony under the trees, he stepped out and looked at them.

'Whom seek ye?' he asked.

'Jesus the Nazarene,' they answered.

'I am he,' Jesus replied.

He moved towards them. They fell back and bowed to the ground. But Judas stepped forward.

'Hail, Rabbi,' he said, and kissed him.

'Would you betray the Son of Man with a kiss?' cried Jesus. 'Friend,' he went on, 'do that for which thou art come.'

At this Malchus, the high priest's servant, moved forward to arrest him. Peter rushed forward, sword in hand, and with a blow sliced off his ear.

'Put up again thy sword into its place,' said Jesus sternly; 'for all they that take the sword shall perish with the sword.'

Jesus turned to the crowd: 'Are you come out as against a robber with swords and staves to seize me?' Then he added: 'But this is your hour and the power of darkness.'

They now came to him and bound his wrists with a rope. All the disciples fled into the darkness; two remaining hidden among the trees. Young John Mark moved forward: the soldiers plunged at him. He slipped swiftly from his linen wrap and fled naked back to his home, leaving the sheet in the hands of the soldiers.

CHAPTER XVII

THE TRIAL

THE Temple police and the soldiers led Jesus up the hill towards the palace of the old priest, Annas. Hidden in the shadows, John and Peter followed. Judas crept away; his traitor work done, but already with remorse wringing his heart.

When the crowd reached Annas' palace, the woman door-keeper opened the gates, and they all trooped in, John among them, for he was known to the portress. Peter stayed outside. The Roman soldiers marched back to quarters in the Tower of Antony. Some messengers went to tell Caiaphas that the arrest was made. Jesus was led into the presence of Annas.

Jesus' fearless eyes looked straight into the cruel face of Annas, who began craftily to try to get Jesus to say something that would be a lawful reason for charging him before Pilate with a crime calling for a death-sentence. Time was short. It was already well after midnight. Annas and Caiaphas must have Jesus executed before the pilgrims were about in the morning if he was to be as they planned, out of the way before Passover.

Annas' cross-questioning of Jesus drew nothing from him. Jesus knew as well as Annas that the old priest had no legal right to judge him. At last Jesus protested.

'Why do you question me?' he asked. 'I have talked openly before the world. I have taught in places where the Jews come together. I have said nothing in secret. Why question me? Question those who heard me. These witnesses know what I said.'

A Temple gendarme angrily struck Jesus a brutal blow on the face, shouting: 'Is that the way you answer the high priest?'

A stepped Roman street in Jerusalem

'If I have said anything wrong,' Jesus turned and said, 'prove it; but if what I say is true, why do you strike me?'

They bound Jesus again and led him out and up the Roman street to Caiaphas' palace, John and Peter following behind. Again John entered when the police led Jesus in; while Peter stayed outside. Jesus went up the marble steps to Caiaphas' judgement room; John below, warming himself at the fire in an iron basket brazier, could see all that happened. He asked the woman at the gate if she would let Peter in; she did so. As he thanked her, talking with his countrified Galilean accent, she looked into his face and asked: 'Are you also one of this man's disciples?'

'No,' he lied stoutly, 'I am not.'

Did he do this fearing that if he said 'Yes' she would refuse to let him in, and feeling that, once in, he might help his Lord? The woman was not satisfied. The glow of the fire was on his face. She gazed at him and then said once more: 'That fellow was with him too.'

'Woman,' Peter roughly answered, 'I know nothing about him.' But he got away from the glow of the fire. Nothing, however, could stop him from talking. A member of Malchus' family—whose ear Peter had cut off that night—came up threateningly.

'That fellow was with him' he exclaimed. 'He is a Galilean. His speech betrays him. Didn't I see you in the Garden with him?'

Peter furiously and with oaths swore that he knew nothing of Jesus. His words reached Jesus' ears. As he spoke a cock, stirred by the first approach of dawn, crowed. Jesus' words flashed into his memory. 'Before the cock crows you will have denied me thrice.' He looked up to where Jesus stood before his accusers. Jesus' eyes were on him in sorrowful love. Peter made for the gate and, hurrying out, broke down utterly, his strong body shaken with sobbing. For he had denied his Lord—and would never see him again before his death.

In front of Jesus sat Caiaphas in his marble chair. The bearded Sanhedrin sat in a semicircle, most of them wishing Jesus' death; but at least two members, Nicodemus and a rich scholar named Joseph of Arimathaea, believed in Jesus. Neither of them, however, had the courage needed for taking the supreme step of defending him, for that would have ended their careers.

Caiaphas called witnesses. One asserted this of Jesus; another that; but their evidence did not agree. Several agreed that they had heard him talk about destroying the Temple and rebuilding in three days one not made with hands; but they squabbled as to whether he said, 'I will destroy', or 'I can destroy', the Temple. And, in any case, this was no charge on which to bring him before Pilate for a death-sentence. Jesus did not even trouble to tell them what he had said, which was 'Destroy this temple, and in three days I will rebuild it'; by which, of course, he meant that in place of that great mass of stone and wood, he would begin his invisible world temple, the Kingdom of God in the hearts of men.

The trial was now at an end; for no witnesses agreed and, according to Hebrew law, no man could be condemned to death on his own evidence. Caiaphas, frantic at the notion of failing after all, stood up and challenged Jesus.

'Do you,' he asked, 'make no answer to what these witnesses bring against you?'

Jesus stood silent. Caiaphas then charged Jesus, by the most solemn of all oaths, to answer the greatest of all questions.

'I charge you by the living God that you tell us whether you are the Christ, the Son of God.'

Tense silence held the court. All eyes were on Jesus.

'I am.'

Caiaphas, ignoring the sacred principles of Jewish law, and rending his robe as in horror at the blasphemy, cried: 'What further need have we of witnesses? What other evidence do we need?'

He was full of joy. By Jewish law blasphemy was to be punished by death; and by claiming to be the Son of God Jesus was in their eyes guilty of it. But the death-sentence could only be pronounced by the Roman Procurator. They must persuade Pilate, and that quickly.

Caiaphas sent messengers and made ready to lead him to Pilate. The court-police, seeing this condemned Galilean workman defenceless, spat in his face, gave him blows on the head, and then blindfolded him, hitting him with the flat of their hands and laughing as they cried: 'Prophesy now, you Christ! Tell us who struck you!'

The dawn of Friday, the day before the Passover, was now breaking. Jesus was gripped by police officers and hurried through the streets west of the Temple up the slope towards the Tower of Antony. About a hundred yards south of it they came to an open piazza. It was called Gabbatha—or the Pavement. Looking on to this open space was the Praetorium of the Roman Governor. A balcony ran along the front, shaded by a colonnade. A messenger from Caiaphas went up the steps of this balcony and into the Palace. His message was that the high priest had a prisoner to be condemned to death, and asking Pilate to come out and deliver the sentence, for Caiaphas could not enter the polluted heathen Praetorium, as it would defile him so that he could not take the Passover at sunset that day.

Pilate, cross at being called out so early, put on his creamy toga with its purple border and took up his ivory rod of office. So he came to the balcony and looked out on the piazza.

'What accusation have you to bring against this man?' he demanded.

Caiaphas, with great rudeness, retorted: 'If the man were not a criminal we would not have handed him over to you.'

'Take him yourselves and sentence him according to your law,' replied Pilate, who had had bitter experience of meddling with Jewish affairs.

'We have no right to put any one to death,' replied Caiaphas. 'We found this fellow,' he continued, 'leading our nation astray, forbidding the payment of taxes to Caesar, and claiming to be King, the Messiah.'

Pilate distrusted Caiaphas, with good reason. As judge, he knew that his own duty was to find out the facts about Jesus and to give this man, who had no one to defend him, every chance. He beckoned Jesus to come. So Jesus went up on to the balcony and into the judgement hall. Pilate seated himself in his chair of justice. He tackled at once the three charges that Caiaphas had made. As to the first, leading astray the Jewish people, that was not Pilate's business, nor worthy of a death-sentence. As to the question of payment of taxes to Caesar, a score of witnesses could prove that Jesus said the exact opposite of what Caiaphas had declared that he said. Pilate went straight to the third charge, which was important to himself as ruler under Rome in Palestine.

'Then you are the King of the Jews, are you?' asked Pilate. Jesus answered with a question that threw Pilate's mind back again on Caiaphas' untrustworthiness.

'Are you saying that of your own accord, or did others tell you that about me?'

'Am I a Jew?' exclaimed Pilate. 'Your own nation and the high priests have handed you over to me. What have you done?' he asked. Jesus at once struck straight to the heart of what Pilate rightly needed to know—was he a rebel against Rome?

'My Kingdom,' he said, 'is not of this world. If my Kingdom were of this world my men would have fought with all their might to stop me from being handed over to the rulers. No, my Kingdom lies elsewhere.'

Pilate had ceased to believe in the ancient gods and goddesses of Rome. Jesus' picture of the invisible Kingdom of the Spirit gave him a glimpse of a new faith. He wanted Jesus to go on.

'So you *are* a King,' he said.

'What you say is true, I am a King,' Jesus replied. 'For that was I born and came into the world—to witness for the truth. Every one who is on the side of truth listens to my voice.'

'Truth,' Pilate echoed Jesus' word. 'What is truth?' he exclaimed. He would happily have sat listening to some word from Jesus on that; but Pilate the ruler and judge now pushed aside Pilate the philosopher. His judicial mind told him that it was mad to think of this gentle and dignified peasant, with his winning talk about a Kingdom of Spirit and of Truth, as a dangerous revolutionary.

Leaving Jesus, he strode out. He gave judgement that Jesus was innocent!

'I find no crime in him,' Pilate declared.

Again the trial was over. Jesus was acquitted by the highest court in the land. Caiaphas, baffled, was not beaten. He set his will to wear down Pilate, whose weakness he already knew. He started the mob of temple-followers shouting.

'He stirs up the people,' they yelled, 'teaching all through Judaea. He began in Galilee. Now he is here.'

'Is this man a Galilean?' asked Pilate, feeling for a way of escape.

'Yes,' they answered.

'Then he is under Herod Antipas' rule,' said Pilate. These two loathed one another. But Pilate was eager to slip out of responsibility for a case that might be heard of in Rome itself. So he ordered Jesus to be led to the citadel that Herod the Great had built, where his son Antipas was now staying during the feast. A messenger ran ahead to tell Herod. He was overjoyed. He had long wished to see this prophet. Was he, as some said, John the Baptist, whom he had beheaded, come to life again? Would he work a miracle? Jesus came before Herod. To all his inquiries Jesus made no reply. But Herod clearly saw that there was no ground for a death-sentence. The oriental despot in him decided to make sport of Jesus. A slave dragged an old robe of Herod's out of a chest. Putting it on Jesus, they jeered at him as at a mock king.

As Pilate waited in the judgement hall for Herod's verdict, a messenger came from his own wife. She had just been awakened, for it was still barely seven o'clock in the morning, from a terrifying dream. Her maidens told her of the trial that Pilate was engaged in. Swiftly writing on her wax tablet, she sent this message to her husband.

'Do nothing with that innocent man. I have suffered much this morning in a dream concerning him.'

As Pilate read this, Jesus came back from Herod with the royal robes over his shoulders. A messenger brought word that Herod saw nothing to condemn in him. Pilate again went to the balcony overlooking the Pavement. The mob grew silent.

'You brought this man before me as an inciter to rebellion among the people. I have examined him before you. I have found nothing criminal about him, in spite of all your accusations against him. No, nor has Herod, for he has sent him back to us. He has done nothing, you see, that is worthy of death.

'I will free him with a scourging,' he concluded.

Caiaphas and his priests at once led the mob in a yell of protest.

'Crucify him: crucify him,' they shouted, clamouring for

the cruel method of killing convicts that the Romans used for slaves and rebels.

'You have a custom,' replied Pilate, 'that I should release to you each year at the Passover one prisoner. Shall I release to you the King of the Jews?'

'No,' surged the reply; 'not this man, but Barabbas.' Barabbas was a highway-robber.

Pilate, still wanting to free Jesus, but anxious to please the mob, gave orders to scourge him. His back was bared and a soldier lashed him with a whip whose leather thongs were weighted with bits of lead and iron. Most people lashed with it were driven mad by the agony, if they did not die. Unbinding him from the pillar to which he was tied for the scourging, they flung Herod's robe over him again and plaited the thorn-twigs used for lighting the fire into a mock crown which they pressed on his head. Some-one seized a bulrush from a vase and thrust it into his hand as a mock sceptre. Then they smote him on the face, crying: 'Hail, King of the Jews.'

Pilate went out on to the balcony to the crowd again, with Jesus.

'See, I am bringing him out to you. I find no crime in him. Behold the man!'

Jesus stood there in his mock royal robes and crown and with his sceptre, kingly, and with unbroken courage amid the howling of the mob and the cruelty of the soldiers.

'Crucify him; crucify him;' the mob battered Pilate's ears with the shouting.

Pilate's will was weakening, as Caiaphas knew it would.

'Take him and crucify him yourselves,' he said.

'We have a law,' Caiaphas called back, 'and by that law he is bound to die, because he has made himself out to be the Son of God.'

Pilate winced. His wife's dream! Was it possible that, after all, it was so? He led Jesus back again.

'Whence do you come?' he asked.

Jesus kept silence. He saw the weakness of Pilate, his desire to curry favour with the Jewish authorities so that there should be no deputations sent to the Emperor behind his back to ruin his career.

'You will not reply,' exclaimed Pilate. 'Do you not know that it is in my power to release you or to crucify you?'

'You would have no power over me,' Jesus answered, 'had it not been given you from above. For that reason, he who gave me up is more guilty than you are.'

Pilate was clearer than ever that he ought to free Jesus. He walked to the parapet of the balcony to say so. Caiaphas shot his last bolt.

'If you set him free you are no friend of Caesar's. Any one who makes himself a king is a rebel against Caesar.'

It was a scarcely veiled threat that, if Pilate freed Jesus, the high priest would complain to the Emperor Tiberius. Pilate made one last gesture. He set Jesus in a marble chair.

'Behold your King,' he said.

'Off with him; away with him!' they howled. 'Crucify him!'

'Crucify your King?' Pilate demanded.

'We have no king save Caesar,' replied Caiaphas.

Pilate told a slave to bring him a basin of water. He rinsed his hands in it. It was a stupid climax to his flabby cowardice.

'I am innocent of this good man's blood. It is your affair.'

But he could not really get rid of his responsibility to administer justice firmly.

'His blood be on us and on our children,' shouted the priests and the mob drunk with their cruel success.

Pilate gave Jesus to them to be crucified, and set Barabbas, the highway-robber, free.

CHAPTER XVIII

VICTORY

Two beams were picked out of the store and nailed cross-wise. A Roman scribe, with brown paint and a brush, inscribed on an oblong board, in the three languages used in Jerusalem—Hebrew, Greek, and Latin—words dictated by Pilate:

JESUS OF NAZARETH
KING OF THE JEWS

A herald carried this board and stood with it in front of Jesus on whose shoulder the cross was laid for him to carry it to the rocky hill outside the city wall, where he was to be crucified. The priests strode angrily towards the balcony and called for Pilate.

'Do not write "King of the Jews",' they protested, 'but, he said, "I am the King of the Jews".'

'What I have written, I have written,' growled Pilate.

The priests now departed to the Temple to take their part in the sacrifices at the altar of the Most High God! For that evening was the Passover supper and many thousands of lambs were to be slain. The priests in the Holy Place were startled to see a haggard man with wild eyes rush towards them. He hurled thirty pieces of silver on the marble pavement.

'I have sinned; I have sinned,' he moaned; 'I have betrayed innocent blood.'

'What is that to us?' said the priests.

So Judas hastened out; but the fact haunted him, that the Lord whom he had loved was now being nailed to a cross to die—betrayed by himself. What had goaded him to do it? Tortured with remorse, Judas hanged himself.

Jesus was now moving slowly up the slope to Golgotha, the Hill of a Skull. On his bent shoulder was the weight of the cross. For thirty hours he had had no sleep. The trial before Annas and then Caiaphas, Pilate, and Herod; the scourging and the brutal horseplay of the soldiers had drained his strength. He staggered under the weight of the cross and fell, fainting.

A muscular Jew from North Africa, named Simon, who was standing there, was told by the Roman officer to carry the cross behind Jesus. A multitude of pilgrims now thronged the way. They were quite different from the Jerusalem mob that had clamoured for Jesus to be crucified, which was made up of people who cringed to the Temple priests. Now the pilgrims from all over the Jewish world began to be about in the streets and they, as we have seen, were on the side of Jesus. Women wept aloud.

Some women always came to the place of crucifixion carrying wine drugged with myrrh in order to deaden the pain of the criminals. They offered this to Jesus before the nails were driven through his hands and feet to nail him to the cross. He would not drink it; for he willed to face death with mind clear and spirit alert.

The four soldiers whose work it was to crucify him, stripped his seamless robe from his back. When his feet and hands were nailed to the cross, he cried out: 'Father, forgive them, for they know not what they do.'

So the four soldiers lifted the cross with Jesus on it and set it in the socket cut for it in the rock of that hill-top.

The soldiers at the foot of the cross, seeing that his was a seamless robe, did not wish to tear it in four pieces, and so threw dice to see which should have it for himself.

'Boaster,' jeered some passers-by, looking up at Jesus, 'you who can destroy the Temple and build it in three days; if you are the Son of God, come down from the Cross.'

'He saved others,' sneered some priests, 'himself he cannot save.'

As the soldiers heard the jeers, they thought that they would join in. They drank the health of 'the King' in mockery, in the sour wine that was the only drink allowed them while on duty.

'If thou art the King of the Jews, save thyself,' they jeered.

One of the thieves who were crucified, one on either side of Jesus, joined in these taunts: 'Art thou not the Christ? Then save thyself and us as well.'

'Hast thou no fear of God,' cried the other thief to his fellow criminal, 'now that thou art under the same punishment? And we justly so, for we only get what we deserve; but this man has done nothing wrong.'

With that he turned to Jesus, and said: 'Do not forget me when thou shalt have come into thy Kingdom.'

'I tell you,' replied he, 'thou shalt be with me this day in Paradise.'

While these things were taking place, crowds of pilgrims, drawn by the rumour of the crucifixion of Jesus, came hurrying to the place, full of sadness. As though the very sky shared their grief, darkness covered the earth about midday; and three hours later a sudden, short earthquake tremor shook Jerusalem, rending the curtain that hid the Holy Place in the Temple.

Slowly the disciples, bewildered and heart-broken, came together at some distance from the cross, watching. All was at an end for them. Jesus was dying. The Kingdom of God had not come. The wolves had slain the Good Shepherd and his flock was scattered. He had often warned them of what lay ahead: but their minds were so full of the hope of a Messiah triumphant over all his enemies, that they could not grasp the truth. And no wonder. Who ever heard of a leader being slain as a criminal and yet being victorious?

John took the hand of Mary, Jesus' Mother, and led

her up the rocky incline to the foot of the cross. Mary of Magdala and Mary the wife of Cleopas followed. Jesus' strength was now ebbing. He looked with love on John and Mary.

'O woman,' he said to his mother, 'behold thy son.'

'O son,' he said to John, 'behold thy mother.'

From that hour John took her into his home.

'I thirst,' Jesus said.

A soldier took a small sponge, used for a cork in their bottle of sour unfermented wine. He soaked it, set it on the point of his javelin, and lifted it to Jesus' lips. In that hour Jesus was utterly alone. Out of the depths Jesus cried: 'My God, my God, why didst thou forsake me?'

That cry to God was the beginning of a Psalm that Jesus had learned as a boy; a song that rose at the end to triumph. As he hung there, words from another song of his boyhood came to his lips: 'Father, into Thy hands I commend my spirit.'

'It is finished,' he said; and his head bowed, as he gave up his spirit.

Seeing that he was dead, his disciples and the many pilgrims who believed in him turned and went back to the city, beating their breasts with grief.

'This man was beyond question innocent,' said a Roman centurion who had stood watching him.

Two members of the Sanhedrin were also watching at a distance and making plans. They were Nicodemus and Joseph of Arimathaea. They now hurried into Jerusalem.

Joseph had, some time before, had a tomb prepared for himself in the orchard close by; and he had secretly been a disciple of Jesus in his heart, although afraid to confess this openly. His friend, Nicodemus, hastened to the bazaar and bought a large quantity of myrrh and the wood of aloes for embalming the Lord's body. Joseph, equally swiftly, strode to the Praetorium to seek audience of Pilate.

On the way to the tomb

'I wish the body of Jesus,' he said when admitted to the presence, 'to give him burial in a tomb that I own.'

Pilate sent a running messenger to Golgotha to discover if Jesus were really dead. The centurion on duty came to Pilate from the place of crucifixion. 'He has been dead for some time,' he said.

So Pilate gave permission. Joseph hurried away; for at sunset Caiaphas would have been able to have Jesus' body taken and thrown on the fire of Gehenna, the rubbish-fire that was always burning. Joseph bought a roll of fine linen. With it he went to the cross, which was taken down. Jesus was lifted from it. The women drew near and helped to swathe his body in this new linen sheet and his head in separate wrappings. Putting about him the spices so that they might after Passover embalm his body, the men carried him to Joseph's tomb that was cut in the side of the rock, followed by the three Marys—his mother, the Magdalene, and the mother of James. The men rolled the circular flat stone against the face of the tomb. It was sunset.

The Sabbath Passover began. Through that night and all through the following day and night, the disciples mourned and faced the tragedy and failure that had broken all their hopes.

The third day dawned. Mary of Magdala and Mary, the mother of James, were already afoot and on the way to the tomb before the sky was light, to begin to embalm him.

'How shall we move that great stone from the tomb?' they wondered. Arriving there they were astounded. The stone was rolled away. A young man in white sat there. They were in terror.

'Fear not,' he said. 'You look for Jesus of Nazareth? He is not here; he is risen. Go; give his disciples and especially Peter this message: "He goes ahead of you to Galilee. You shall see him there." '

The women hastened back to the upper room where the disciples were. The men could hardly grasp their breathless story. One thing was clear. The women said that Jesus was risen. Peter and John hastened away to see if this were really true. John, the younger and faster, reached the tomb first; looked in and saw the cloths on the ground. Peter, more daring, went right into the tomb. There were the linen cloths that had been bound about Jesus, with the head-cloths folded separately; but the Lord was gone. Peter called to John; he plucked up his courage, went in, saw, and believed.

Mary of Magdala had hurried back to the tomb. Peter and John went back to tell the others; she stayed, watching and weeping.

'Woman,' a voice said to her, 'why are you weeping?'

'Because they have taken away my Master,' she said, looking up and seeing a Man dimly through her tears.

He asked her the same question, but still she did not recognize him.

'Oh, sir,' she exclaimed, 'if you have carried him away, tell me where you have put him. I will remove him.'

'Mary,' he said. At the sound of her own name in the familiar voice, she swiftly moved to him with hands outstretched, grasping at his arm.

'Do not touch me,' he said. 'Go to my brothers and tell them, "I am ascending to my Father and yours, to my God and yours."'

She flew back to Jerusalem as swiftly as her feet could carry her.

'I have seen the Master,' she cried as she burst in upon them, 'I have seen him.'

They could hardly believe her words, and thought pityingly that her grief had given her delusions.

That afternoon two disciples, Cleophas and a friend, set out from Jerusalem to their home in Emmaus, a village eight miles south-west from the city on the Roman road.

As they walked along they talked of nothing but Jesus' death, and the death of all their hopes of the Kingdom of God. A stranger joined them.

'What is this that you are talking about as you walk?' he asked.

'Are you a stranger, living all alone in Jerusalem,' cried Cleophas, 'that you know nothing of the things that have been happening?'

'What things?' he inquired.

'About Jesus of Nazareth,' they replied. 'In the eyes of God and of all the people he was a prophet great in deeds and words; but the high priests and the government gave him up to be sentenced to death. For ourselves we hoped that he would be the redeemer of Israel; but he is dead three days ago. Though,' they added, 'some women among our number were at the tomb early this morning and came to tell us that they had seen angels who said that he was alive. Some of our brethren found it just as they had said, but him they did not see.'

'O dull-witted men,' said the stranger, 'and slow of heart to believe all that the prophets have spoken. Was it not necessary that the Christ should suffer thus, and so enter into his glory?'

So he recalled what Moses, Isaiah, and the other prophets had said. He showed them that what they had thought was the end of all, might, indeed, be but the beginning of new life for them and the world.

As they talked they entered Emmaus. Cleophas and his friend stopped by their little home that lay on the left-hand side of the Roman road. Jesus moved on.

'See, it is towards evening,' they said, pointing to the lengthening shadows; 'stay with us.'

He went into the little house and they reclined at supper

in the flickering, uncertain light of the wall lamps. He took bread, and, breaking it, said a blessing. In a flash they knew him. But Jesus went from their sight.

'Did not our hearts glow within us,' they said, 'as he talked with us on the road, opening the Scripture to us.'

They could not stay; they must share their glorious news. Their sandals were soon on and away they hurried northward in the swiftly fading twilight. In two hours they were again in the upper room. As they shared their experience the others cried: 'The Master has risen and has appeared to Simon.'

What the Lord said to Peter and he to Jesus we cannot know; but the wilful disciple, who had denied his Lord, went on from that day through all his life to his own crucifixion with daring loyalty that never failed. As the disciples in the upper room shared their experiences, a familiar voice said the words that are always spoken in the East on entering a home: 'Peace be with you.' This time, however, they meant something new and wonderful to the men and women who thought that peace would never again visit them. He showed them the prints of the nails that had pierced his hands and his feet and in his side a wound where a soldier had struck with his spear.

'Peace be with you!' said Jesus again. 'As the Father sent me, even so I send you forth. Receive the Holy Spirit.'

So he left them. Thomas the Twin was not there. When he came back and they eagerly told him the news, he refused to believe it. They must be deluded.

'Unless I see the marks of the nails and put my fingers on the marks, I will not believe.'

On the first day of the week, seven days later, they were again together in the upper room.

'Peace be with you,' said the voice. Jesus was with them again. He beckoned to Thomas.

'Put your finger here; look. Do not refuse to believe, but believe.'

'My Master,' cried Thomas, 'and my God.'

'Is it because you have seen me that you believe?' said Jesus. 'Blessed are they who have not seen, yet have believed.'

He went again from their sight. Peter recalled that Jesus had sent the message to them by the young man in the Empty Tomb that he would meet them in Galilee. So the Twelve walked the familiar way northward, but without their Master. Jesus was, indeed, in Galilee before them and spoke there to his brother James, who had been unfriendly to him, but who now became a follower of Jesus Christ and became the leader of all the disciples who, in the years to come, lived in Jerusalem.

Peter grew restless: he wanted to feel a fishing-net in his hand, the restless swing of the boat on the water, and the tug of the sail in the breeze.

'I go a fishing,' he said. With him went James and John, Thomas and Nathanael, and two others. Peter, in the hot night of early summer, down in the trough of Jordan, threw off his clothing. So they toiled at their fishing; but they had no luck. Dawn broke. They were near the shore.

'Fellows,' a voice came across the water, 'have you any fish?'

'No,' they replied.

'Cast your net to starboard and you will find fish.'

They did so. As they hauled at the net, it was so heavy with fish that the seven men could not pull it in.

'It is the Lord,' cried John, whose brain was swifter and more sensitive than Peter's. Peter, to whom action was easier than thought, caught up his tunic, flung it on, leapt over the side of the boat, and plunged through the water to the shore; the first to reach his Master. The others, pulling ashore in the dinghy, dragged the net. Already a fire was alight.

'Bring some of the fish that you have caught,' Jesus said.

Peter went to help. The net held a hundred and fifty-three fish; and its fine thread was not torn. Jesus grilled the fish and once more the Eleven comrades and their Lord were together in the open air by the lake that they loved.

'Simon, son of John,' said Jesus, turning to Peter, 'dost thou love me more than the others do?'

'Why, Lord?' exclaimed his wondering disciple, 'Thou knowest that I love thee!'

'Feed my lambs,' said Jesus.

After a silence, he asked again: 'Simon, son of John, dost thou love me?'

'O Lord, thou knowest that I love thee,' Peter said.

'Feed my sheep,' Jesus said.

After a moment's silence, Jesus a third time tested his disciple: 'Simon, son of John, do you love me?'

It pained Peter, who remembered how he had three times denied that he knew Jesus. That his Master should a third time ask, 'Do you love me?'

'Master,' he said, 'thou knowest all things; thou knowest that I love thee.'

'Feed my sheep,' said Jesus again. 'Truly, I tell thee, thou hast put round thee thine own girdle and walked whither thou wouldst in the days of thy youth, but when thou art old, thou shalt stretch out thine hands for others to gird thee, and thou shalt be taken whither thou wouldst not go.'

Jesus was showing Peter the road along which he was to face whatever adventure should befall him in carrying across the seas, even to Rome, the Good News of the love of God in Jesus Christ, and at the end of that road was a cross. In that road and in face of all peril the one power that was to keep him strong was his love of Jesus of whose strength he had thrice questioned Peter. Yet, even now, Peter must blurt out a question that was not his concern. He asked what was to happen to his friend John. Jesus told him that this did not concern him. What did matter was that he should obey the command that Jesus had given to him and to Andrew on the same lake-side at the beginning of their fellowship with him: 'Follow thou me.'

Jesus told them to meet him once more on the familiar hill-top where they had again and again shared such comradeship. On that high place he had chosen them; he had taught them there, and had sent them out two by two to their own nation. At this last time that he would meet them there he sent them on a quest that has never ceased.

'Go and make disciples of all nations; and teach them to obey all the commands that I have given you. And, lo, I will be with you all the days, even unto the end of the world.'

INDEX